The Inner War

The Inner War

Forms and Themes in Recent American Poetry

Paul A. Lacey

Fortress Press   Philadelphia

To Margie, Mary, Patrick and James—

without whom everything is prose

Contents

Preface

I want to celebrate the good influences which have helped me write this book. First there was the steady skillful help of the staff of Earlham College's Lilly Library. Mary Linkhart ordered books from the most out-of-the-way places and got them when I needed them. Leo Chang, James Kennedy, and Philip Shore helped me with difficult research problems. Evan and Hope Farber brought their own interest and wide reading to my aid. From all those friends I received not only the professional help I requested but the benefit of their continued interest in my project, expressed in the way they called poems, articles, and books to my attention and ordered works they thought I could use.

Three of my colleagues, John W. Hunt, Leigh T. Gibby, and Douglas L. Eichhorn, have given me confidence by the warmth of their response to earlier drafts of the book. Each has also performed that greater service to a friend, pointing out flaws before they get committed to print. Sister Sarah Fahy, S.N.D., and Sister Patricia McNeal, S.S.N.D., read and commented on the chapter on William Everson and Barbara Miles Levine read the chapter on Anne Sexton. I gladly record my affectionate thanks to them.

I am indebted to a number of groups and individuals whose response to the poets and my writing about them helped sharpen and clarify my understanding. I recall with special pleasure a seminar in literary criticism in 1968, where Peter Berliner, Patricia Lorton, James Mitchell, and James Wallace read Robert Bly's poetry with me. One of them still owes me a paper, from which I hereby absolve him. A week-end seminar at Powell House, a Quaker retreat center in Old Chatham, New York, and a lecture series at Friends General Conference in 1970 both gave me opportunities to try out my ideas on nonacademic audiences.

PREFACE

A lecture to the Indiana Academy of Religion on Robert Bly and one to the Phi Beta Kappa chapter at Earlham College on Denise Levertov in 1971 gave me further valuable experience. Each such chance for discussion has enriched my understanding of the poetry and, I believe, improved the book.

Earlham College gave me a sabbatical leave in 1969–70 and a grant from the Humanities Faculty Development Fund (supported by the Ford Foundation), so I might have leisure to study and write. For this and a great deal more I owe special thanks to the help and friendship of Dean Joe Elmore.

The typing was done by Rosemary Wesler and Evelyn Sharvin from copy which taxed their ingenuity and patience.

As good influences go deeper they become harder to define. I mention only three. My companions in the search for the future of the Quaker movement did not influence the book directly, but every word and idea owes something to those years of our close association at Pendle Hill. They are part of my ideal audience, as I am part of theirs. In like fashion, those colleagues with whom I wasted time in good talk in the faculty lounge when we all should have been tending to business have enriched the book by enriching me. Finally, there are my wife and children who, if the truth be told, not only did not help me finish the book but probably slowed it down by some months. But that these have been the happiest years of my life I owe to them.

Witnesses to the Spiritual

This book began as a fishing expedition. Two very different questions engaged my attention. First, what have contemporary poets to say about the spiritual state of our world, what kind of critique of our culture does their work offer and how might it throw light on similar problems being examined by theologians and religious thinkers? That question pursued essentially a thematic line, anticipating that the theologians and poets would speak to one another and to the student who read them together. The second line of inquiry asked about the forms being developed or exploited by the poets. What were the vital forms? How did they relate to the vigorous inventions of the earlier generation of modern poetry in English—Yeats, Eliot, Stevens, Auden, and Lowell? What are the relations of form to content in contemporary American poetry?

If the book had a thesis, it was so general as to receive immediate assent: that poets use form as ways to explore the problems of their time—existential problems, problems of faith and action—but that their themes and discoveries are fresh only because they grow out of the exploration of form and technique. Robert Creeley's famous dictum, "Form is never more than the extension of content," has been modified by Denise Levertov to say, "Form is never more than the revelation of content." Trying to understand the relation of form and content by a close reading of a great many contemporary American poets has given me the insights I try to share in the following chapters.

I have written about five poets moving into their middle years. Only one, James Wright, has published his *Collected Poems*, and that came out while this book was being written. These five poets are still in process, growing in skill, finding new tones of voice, testing their art against a swiftly changing political and social world. The borders are shifting even as I write; half a dozen major works came from these authors in the time since the book was undertaken. William Everson, Brother Antoninus, left the monastic life while I was writing the chapter devoted to his work. The Vietnam War and political unrest in the United States have given new directions to the work especially of Robert Bly and Denise Levertov. More than most books, this one runs the risk of being dated when it leaves the press, but the risk seems worthwhile, for this generation of poets repays close reading. As they come into their full power, the poets of the 1960s and 70s make us know that we are in a new time, with new themes and metaphors, new aesthetics, new attempts to speak of the world we know.

The poetry of the 1950s, at least that poetry which the academic was trained to take seriously, still pursued the strategies of Pound and Eliot. It sought to order experience through tight poetic forms; it made its commentaries on society through the ironic use of classical mythology, literary allusions, and dense symbolism. Poets and critics spoke of the mask, the persona, objectivity to describe the appropriate attitude of detachment from one's poetry. The New Criticism, stressing the values of irony and ambiguity in poetry, also sought to establish the significance of works and writers by linking them with "the tradition." *Modern Poetry and the Tradition*, Cleanth Brooks's fine reading of modern poetry, sets the tone in its very title. Ellmann and Feidelson's *The Modern Tradition*, by the yoking of words which another generation would find contradictory, reminds us of the presuppositions of the previous generation of writers.

When Donald M. Allen published *The New American Poetry: 1945–1960*, in which both Denise Levertov and Brother Antoninus are represented, it was to challenge "the tradition," especially as it had found its home in academic verse. Allen announced a new avant-garde, "the true continuers of the modern movement," poets based in San Francisco and New York; identified with *Origin* and *Black Mountain Review*, *Evergreen Review*, or with The Poet's Theatre, the Artists' Theatre and the Living Theatre; called by names like "the Black Mountain School," "the Beat Generation," "the New York Poets," "the San Francisco Renaissance."

WITNESSES TO THE SPIRITUAL

Each of the poets considered here has been identified by the critics with some "school" of poetry: William Everson with the San Francisco Renaissance and Beat Poetry; Denise Levertov with Black Mountain; James Wright and Robert Bly with poetry of the "subjective image"; Anne Sexton with "confessional poetry." Through his criticism and the example of his own poetry, Robert Bly also seems to be a candidate for having a "school" named after himself. These shorthand labels offer a certain convenience in identifying typical styles and concerns and in distinguishing the newer poets from the previous generation, but they conceal at least as much as they reveal about the particular problems a poet meets as he pursues his work. I have tried to make do, therefore, with very few labels in discussing these poets, preferring instead to look closely at their works to discern what lines of development they evidence. Neither have I tried to study influence in order to show how *this* came out of *that*. When I have followed works back to influences and sources it has been to steep myself in the poems, to follow the leads because the poems recommend their sources. One does not look at a Sligo landscape in order to prove that Yeats saw it right. The poem may recommend the landscape or the landscape the poem, but each makes its own impact. We love each for itself. So with the poetry I have considered and its sources or influences. It has sent me to the Bible, the mystics, Trakl, Neruda, Rilke, Chinese poetry, haiku, Zen, Buber, Boehme, to delight in them for their own sakes. The world has widened for me through this reading, and I try to bring this widened experience to my discussion of the poetry.

The poetry considered here reflects three emphases found widely in American poetry in the 1960s: a preoccupation with the inner world of the psyche and its relation to the world of everyday existence; a revaluation of the imagination as the faculty of discovery and creation; and a blurring of lines which have separated the poem from such other kinds of writing as the notebook, diary, documentary, history, or confession.

Exploring the inner world has led poets into two directions, either plunging into psychological torment, or even Rimbaud's "derangement of the senses" through the use of mind-expanding drugs, and making poetry out of discovering the nature and limits of an individual self; or a turning to the writings of mystics and seers, to psychologists like C. G. Jung and Georg Groddeck, writers like Hesse, Rilke, Trakl, Neruda, primitive myths or eastern religious texts, or the masters and poets of

China and Japan. This second way of looking inward discovers links between the self and other selves, between the self and the universe. "The live world," Bly calls it. When poets go deep enough into the psyche they bring back news of the universe, he says, news of a world of meaning in which man has his part. What follows, then, is a look outward, but from a new perspective, a criticism of society often expressed in political dissent, especially resistance to the Vietnam War, and concern for the environment and the quality of life. Gary Snyder calls one of his books *Earth Household*, a literal translation of "ecology." In a note to his book *The Morning Glory*, Bly says, "There is an old occult saying: whoever wants to see the invisible must penetrate more deeply into the visible. Everything has a right to exist. If we examine an animal carefully, we see how independent it is of us. Its world is complete without us. We feel separated at first; later, joyful." And he quotes with approbation Basho's poem:

> The morning glory—
> Another thing
> That will never be my friend.

The look inward has fostered a deepened interest in the spiritual disciplines of solitude, simplicity, silence, and meditation, both for their own sakes and as aids to the writing of poetry. Poetry itself is once again spoken of as a spiritual discipline. Denise Levertov speaks of meditation, musing, and waiting for inspiration in describing how she writes. William Everson speaks of the muse as *Sophia*, Holy Wisdom bringing her revelation to the poet. For them, the language of religious experience offers the only adequate way to describe what it is like to make poetry.

"A religious devotion to the truth, to the splendor of the authentic," says Denise Levertov, "involves the writer in a process rewarding in itself; but when that devotion brings us to undreamed abysses and we find ourselves sailing slowly over them and landing on the other side— that's ecstasy." The poet's main job, says Bly in "Leaping Up Into Political Poetry," his introduction to an anthology called *Forty Poems Touching on Recent American History*, is to penetrate the husk around the psyche by a sudden drive inward. "Once inside the psyche, he can speak of inward and political things with the same assurance. . . . What is needed to write good poems about the outward world is inwardness."

WITNESSES TO THE SPIRITUAL

A generation ago, T. S. Eliot wanted to describe the poet's mind as a catalytic agent in the presence of which the separate elements interfused to become a poem, and James Joyce has Stephen Dedalus compare the artist to God, completely separate from his creation, detached, paring his fingernails. Those analogies have little currency today. Poets speak again of the work of the imagination, using the word with all the mysterious religious associations which surround it. Bly, speaking of French poetry's "voyage into the imagination," links the imagination to "trust of the animal world, instinctive life, the unconscious."[1]

Denise Levertov identifies the imagination with the creative unconscious and calls it a "holy, independent faculty" whose work is "that *following through*, that *permeation* of detail—relevant, illuminating detail" in a work of art.

> . . . That breathing of life into the dust, is present in us all embryonically—manifests itself in the life of dream—and in that manifestation shows us the possibility: to permeate, to quicken, all of our life and the works we make. What joy to be reminded by truth in dream that the imagination does not arise from the environment but has the power to create it![2]

Robert Kelly says, "The present and necessary function of poetry is the transformation of the perceived world. This transformation orders the known world into an effective and coherent universe. . . ." But he goes on to argue that poetry cannot stop with enlightenment, "Epiphany is meaningless display outside the context of incarnation." "Enlightenment," "redemption," "incarnation"—though there is no way of knowing how seriously Kelly wants to take the theological connotations of the language he uses here, it is clear that seeing and knowing deeply, through the agency of poetry, has enormous importance for him. He associates such knowing with the work of the deep image in "the development of a 'basic imagination'."[3]

It is not accidental that a time which values the creative imagination, creative intuition, intensity, or gusto as means of seeing and making art

1. Robert Bly, "Some Notes on French Poetry," *The Sixties,* no. 5 (Fall 1961): 66–70.
2. Denise Levertov, "A Note on the Work of the Imagination," in *New Directions in Prose and Poetry*, ed. J. Laughlin (New York: New Directions Press, 1961), pp. 48–50.
3. Robert Kelly, "Notes on the Poetry of Deep Image," *Trobar* 2 (1961): 14–16.

should also concern itself with extending the borders of literature to bring in new subjects and new ways to approach material. The Romantics, who gave us such rich speculations on the shaping power of the imagination, the "mighty world of eye and ear, both what they half perceive and half-create," also gave us an understanding of organic form, the artistic work shaped from within by the needs of the material. "The organic form," says Coleridge, "is innate; it shapes as it develops itself from within, and the fullness of its development is one and the same with the perfection of its outward form. Such is the life, such the form."[4] The Romantics also bequeathed us a great range of experiments with form—abandoned projects, noble successes and huge failures, and some works of such power that we are grateful for them even in their incompleteness.

These commonplaces about the Romantics have their application in understanding contemporary poetry. The parallels in political and social events are there; as are the preoccupations with the relation of inwardness to the events of the outward world. The critical vocabularies are also similar, the concern with the imagination and organic form. Most significant however, may be the spirit of experimentation, the voyaging into new materials and ways of writing. Bly, again, speaks of the new way of writing, the new imagination, as a sensitivity to the harmony between form and content. "Form speaks, just as the inner content speaks, but what if they don't say the same thing? Often in America, the poem grunts, and the form speaks in highly polished Cambridge English."[5]

The Times Literary Supplement's reviewer of James Wright's book *Shall We Gather at the River* said it takes us "beyond the normal definitions of literature." Similar comments have been made, or could be, about the work of each of the poets considered here. Anne Sexton's works have been dismissed by some critics for not having successfully transmuted personal experience into finished works of art. They are too close to the experiences which generated them, say James Dickey and Denis Donoghue. Haydon Carruth, reviewing Bly's *The Light Around the Body* says, "In our time the distinction between art and documentation, writing and journalism, poetry and note-keeping, has been persistently narrowed; yet it endures, as it must if we are to justify

4. Terence Hawkes, ed., *Coleridge's Writings on Shakespeare* (New York: Capricorn Books, 1959), p. 68.
5. Robert Bly, "On Current Poetry in America," *The Sixties*, no. 4 (Fall 1960): 28.

ourselves at all. In Bly's little flat poems the distinction has been eroded altogether." William Everson's work has been repeatedly condemned for formlessness and lack of artistic finish. Denise Levertov's *Relearning the Alphabet* certainly invites the same kind of criticism, particularly in several of the longer works. "An Interim" and "From a Notebook: October '68–May '69" splice letters, pamphlets, newspaper stories with the poet's own words into a montage which apparently obliterates the distinctions Carruth insists upon. And Robert Lowell calls his most recent book *Notebook 1967–68*, asking us to read it as "one poem, jagged in pattern."

The blurring of lines between poetry and these other kinds of writing raises a number of questions. What are "the normal definitions of literature"? What do they have to recommend them except their normality or familiarity? How should we distinguish notebook or documentary from art, and why? Will the distinctions be purely formal ones, or is there some content which can never be absorbed into art? Hasn't our experience of life also gone beyond what we have regarded as the normal definitions?

Coleridge says of Shakespeare's poems that the creative power and intellectual energy wrestle in a war embrace but in the plays they were reconciled and fought "each with its shield before the breast of the other." In each of these five poets we see a war embrace of form and content, but we also see reconciliation or its promise, from time to time. And we also see that other inner war to which Denise Levertov refers when she speaks of "Life at War." If the poem grunts, the form must do so, too. What we must hope is that our social and political life can support and justify something more than the grunt of pain, the incoherent lament or cry of despair. "Such is the life, such the form."

The Inner War may seem too melodramatic a title, but what started as a study of the usual tension a poet faces, the intolerable wrestle with words, had to broaden out to a consideration of the inner war which rages in American society and in the lives of millions of Americans. Turning inward can be escapism, and is for many. But it is also a necessary preparation for the turn outward, into effective work in the world. Is this a time of preparation, spiritual deepening, the strengthening of the imagination so that it may produce not poems alone but more humane institutions, ways of living together? The issue of that inner war is in doubt. Our poets may help us discover how to reach the right resolution.

2

The Sacrament of Confession

To distinguish the Robert Lowell of *Life Studies*, Anne Sexton, W. D. Snodgrass, and Sylvia Plath, among others, as "confessional" poets has been useful primarily for calling attention to a subject matter and attitudes toward it. After a generation of criticism which insisted that the "I" of a poem was not to be identified with the writer, the *real* John Keats, T. S. Eliot, or W. B. Yeats, but was to be seen strictly as a persona in the poem, we have returned—in some of our most vital poetry—to first-person utterances which are intended to be taken as autobiographical. Thus M. L. Rosenthal speaks of Lowell's "Skunk Hour" and Sylvia Plath's "Lady Lazarus" as true examples of confessional poetry because "they put the speaker himself at the center of the poem in such a way as to make his psychological vulnerability and shame an embodiment of his civilization,"[1] and he goes on to speak of how the poems show us Lowell's sickness of will and spirit, or Sylvia Plath's self-loathing, leading on to her suicide.

Of course, the relation between the writer and his persona in a poem is still as complex as ever. Though some critics have cited the passage in "Skunk Hour" where the speaker tells of spying on lovers in their cars as evidence of Lowell's illness, the incident, in fact, comes from one of Walt Whitman's letters.[2] Similarly, readers have been so persuaded of the factual foundation for Anne Sexton's "Unknown Girl in the Mater-

---

1. M. L. Rosenthal, *The New Poets: American and British Poetry Since World War II* (New York: Oxford University Press, 1967), p. 79.
2. Robert Lowell, "On 'Skunk Hour'," in *Robert Lowell: A Collection of Critical Essays*, ed. Thomas Parkinson (Englewood Cliffs, N.J.: Prentice-Hall, 1968), p. 133.

nity Ward," that they have assumed the poet herself must have had an illegitimate child—which she has not. The dramatic lyric or monologue still sets up some distance between writer and character; but a new openness, a willingness to make poetry of experience unmediated by such doctrines of objectivity as the mask, the persona, or the objective correlative, a preoccupation with extraordinary experiences—mental breakdown, infidelity, divorce—these are some of the hallmarks of "confessional poetry." And, with deep gratitude for the lessons in close reading taught us by the criticism which insists that we must read each poem as "a little world made cunningly," without reference to biography, history, or the body of work created by the same artist, we must nevertheless apply those lessons in new ways, especially when confronted with writers who consciously refuse to write within that critical canon. "There is always an appeal open from criticism to nature," said Dr. Johnson.

To interest us for very long, poetry must offer more than the *frisson* of shocked pleasure which accompanies our learning that someone else acts out our fantasies; it must be more than a casebook example of abnormal psychology; and it must make more demand on our attention than that—in the words of many novice writers—"this really happened to me!" Which is to say that, whatever the adjective "confessional" tells us about subject matter, the noun it modifies, "poetry," points us once more to the questions of style and form. A poem gives shape to experience so that both the experience itself, in all its density and complexity, with whatever tastes, sights, feelings, and textures are peculiar to it, and the "meanings"—the insights, reflections, consequences, emotional and spiritual implications of the shaped experience—become available to us.

When we write poetry, we do so in order to re-live or celebrate experience, to put things that have happened to us together with others that have not—things we have imagined or appropriated from our reading, our observations, or our friends. But we also write poetry to play with language, to obscure or mediate experiences through words, images, and rhymes. Starting perhaps with an emotion we wish to preserve, we become concerned with how things sound or look, how the rhythm builds or breaks, how emotions are generated and channeled by what we are saying. Looking for release or discovery, we also become interested in making the poem *work*, in saying things well. The poem, then, looks two ways, toward expression and toward communication. It organizes our responses as we write, but it also organizes responses in the audience we begin to imagine.

As readers of poetry we look for the signals from the poem which organize our responses, which tell us we are reading aright and confirm our satisfactions in seeing what is really there. The poem creates its own frame of reference, establishing the norms—ethical, emotional, social, personal—by which we understand it. The poem tells us how to regard its statements, how to read a pattern of metaphors, when the stance is ironic, when it is successfully or unsuccessfully finished. It leads us to make judgments by comparing it with other works in its genre, or with a similar theme or tone.

What organizes our responses, whether we are writing or reading poetry, and leads us to satisfaction or dissatisfaction with the final result, is form, what Robert Frost calls "the figure a poem makes."

> . . . There is a big change after you write a poem. It's a marvelous feeling, and there's a big change in the psyche, but I think you really go into great chaos just before you write a poem, and during it, and then to have come out of that whole, somehow is a small miracle, which lasts for a couple of days. Then on to the next. [3]

The satisfactions Anne Sexton speaks of have to do with moving from and through chaos into wholeness. They are both aesthetic and psychological, both impersonal and highly personal, and they come together in the process of finding adequate form, or, to put it another way, in exerting control over the chaos and making it yield up meaning. "For one lyric poem I rewrote about 300 typewritten pages. . . . You have to look back at all those bad words, bad metaphors, everything stated wrong, and then see how it came into being, the slow progress of it, because you're always fighting to find out what it is you want to say." [4]

The pleasures of writing poetry are not the same as those we antici- pate in reading it, however, and while most poets might speak in a similar fashion about the pains and pleasures of composition, the reader of "confessional" poetry seems faced with a particularly complex set of

3. Patricia Marx, "Interview with Anne Sexton," *Hudson Review* 18, no. 4 (Win- ter 1965–66): 570.
4. Ibid., p. 562.

claims on his responses. What are his satisfactions? What entrée does he have into the poem? If the reader is being addressed in some special "confessional" sense, what is his role? Is he hearing confession like a priest, granting or withholding absolution? Is he the client-victim of such a judge-penitent as the narrator of Camus's *The Fall* or Coleridge's *Ancient Mariner*? Do we overhear an unwitting confession, as we do in "The Bishop Orders His Tomb" or "My Last Duchess"? Or are we suddenly drawn into the life of the poem by a violation of the distance established by the form, as Eliot draws us into the action of "The Waste Land": "You! hypocrite lecteur!—mon semblable,—mon frere!"

Equally important, what protection does the poem offer the reader from too much harrowing, too dangerous an evocation of psychic material within himself? The content of any confession is likely to be threatening to one who hears it. If it occurs in a context where one cannot imitate the detachment of a priest, or where the response demanded is too revealing, one may only withdraw or block all response. A reader is at once the most defenseless and the most powerful of men; he may be moved and manipulated by every intonation and gesture the poet gives, but he may also close the book and go away.

All these are questions which must be raised about most poetry, but asking them about Anne Sexton's poetry leads us directly to problems of poetic form as she has faced them.

It has been relatively easy for some critics to dismiss Anne Sexton's poetry by concentrating on its subject matter. Reviewing her first book, James Dickey begins:

> Anne Sexton's poems so obviously come out of deep, painful sections of the author's life that one's literary opinions scarcely seem to matter; one feels tempted to drop them furtively into the nearest ashcan, rather than be caught with them in the presence of so much naked suffering.[5]

Hayden Carruth speaks of a mind almost in control of her material; Denis Donoghue speaks sympathetically of the experiences Anne Sexton has gone through, but he concludes that she has tried too hard to make the material into poetry. Carruth, again, argues that the literary qualities of her poems are impossible to judge, that they are still documentaries of experience which might be starters for other poems where

5. James Dickey, "Five First Books," *Poetry* 97, no. 5 (February 1961): 318–19.

images and ideas "may be strengthened and consolidated in more fully objectified, imagined poems."[6] Flatness, lack of concentration, an unfinished quality to the poetry, or, alternatively, works which try too hard to be poems: these are the standard criticisms of Anne Sexton's works.

But a careful reading of her four books of poetry reveals, not the lack of form which these critics emphasize, but a continual preoccupation with both thematic and technical means for giving significant shape to her poetry. Many of the poems have elaborate rhyme and metrical patterns. Each of the books is shaped by ruling themes, carefully chosen epigraphs, or a chronological or developmental pattern. The title *To Bedlam and Part Way Back* precisely indicates the arc which the book describes, and which each poem is designed to advance: from sickness toward health; from possession by the ghosts and demons of guilt toward exorcism; from disownment toward inheritance. The book's epigraph describes the method by which the way back can be won: making a clean breast of it in the face of every question; pushing the inquiry further, even in the face of appalling horror.

All My Pretty Ones announces the themes of the book, total loss and the affliction of memory: "I cannot but remember such things were, that were most precious to me." And, just as for Wordsworth recalling emotion and experience under the control of artistic creation brings new health and strength, the aim of remembering for Anne Sexton is to learn to exorcise the evil and celebrate the good. The book's second epigraph, taken from a letter by Franz Kafka, tells us what to expect in the way of method and goal for the poetry, which will "act upon us like a misfortune," and "serve as the ax for the frozen sea within us." The epigraphs do not promise the satisfactions of resolution or the sense of a completed journey. At the most, they promise to take us to the edge of things, the boundary situation, where, for good or ill, the frozen sea within us begins to break up.

Live or Die is the appropriate next stage of development in the poetry. The choice announced by the title is real for the poet, but the poems, printed in the order of their composition from 1962 to 1966, do not simply move from death- to life-wish. "Live or die, but don't poison everything," says the epigraph, and the poems enact the process of throwing off the poison which makes them read, as Anne Sexton

6. Hayden Carruth, "In Spite of Artifice," *Hudson Review* (Winter 1966–67): 698.

says, "like a fever chart for a bad case of melancholy." In the final poem, "Live," she gathers up the ruling words, images, and themes of the book to express a new equilibrium.

> So I won't hang around in my hospital shift,
> repeating the Black Mass and all of it.
> I say *Live, Live* because of the sun,
> the dream, the excitable gift.

Finally, in *Love Poems*, she quotes from a Yeats essay about the teaching of Mohini Chaterjee, "Everything that has been shall be again." The poems affirm the body in a way not to be found in her earlier poetry. Whereas in the first three books the body is apt to be described as a prison cell or a house inhospitable to its occupant, in this last book the whole body and its separate parts are celebrated and delighted in. Images of the lover as architect, builder, and kneader abound. The poetry asserts the creative power of love and is less self-conscious of its own nature. The eternal cycle described by Mohini Chaterjee brings a sense of peace to the poems gathered in this book.

This brief examination of one means by which Anne Sexton has shaped her collections of poems does not argue that carefully chosen titles, epigraphs, and influences will improve or justify a particular poem, any more than showing that a poem is a perfect Petrarchan sonnet or in terza rima proves that it is a successful work. What may be argued from such conscious shaping of her books, however, is first, that we must read and evaluate each poem in its larger context, just as we read each line or extended image of a poem in the context created by the whole poem; and second, that the confessional mode requires such shaping influences to give both the distance and familiarity a reader needs for handling the material. Speaking of *All My Pretty Ones*, May Swenson notes:

> Her method is as uninhibited as entries in a diary or letter . . . ,the diction seems effortless, yet when we examine for form we find it solidly there, and its expertness is a pleasurable thing in contrast to the merciless *debridement* taking place in the content.[7]

Just as any confession must provide signals telling us how to respond and protections from too much danger, confessional poetry must balance horror with comfort, threat with relief, merciless *debridement*

7. May Swenson, "Poetry of Three Women," *Nation* (February 1963): 165–66.

with pleasure, in order to keep us engaged. So the wrenching loss described in "Unknown Girl in the Maternity Ward" and the claustrophobic terror of "The Moss of His Skin" are lightened by the hopeful ritual of "The Lost Ingredient" and the lyrical self-control of "For John, Who Begs Me Not to Enquire Further":

> Not that it was beautiful
> but that I found some order there.
> There ought to be something special
> for someone
> in this kind of hope.

To convince us that we have experienced something true, and that we can live *by* and *with* what we have experienced, is the supreme accomplishment of art. Anne Sexton has said, "I think all form is a trick in order to get at the truth." The remark underlines the importance for her of shaping the lived or imagined experience into the truth. She says in her interview with Patricia Marx that in the poems which are hardest for her to write, she imposes some exceptionally difficult metre or rhyme-scheme, which *allows* her to be truthful. "It works as a kind of super-ego. It says 'You may now face it, because it will be impossible to get out'!"

The *content*, it must be insisted, does not make the poem truthful. Even the most autobiographical poet distorts or suppresses *facts* for the sake of making a fiction which will tell more of the essential truth. To reach its readers, the poem must persuade us that the truth it tells is worth the price it exacts; it must lead us to appropriate and satisfying reactions. Form operates to say to the reader what it says to Anne Sexton: this is a pattern which allows you to be truthful.

The thematic and technical forms she uses in the books establish the distance from the material which allows us first to contemplate it and then to approach it more closely. The Greek tragedians were able to handle the most psychically dangerous material we know—incest, parricide, and matricide—precisely because the stylized language, acting, masks and costumes established sufficient distance between the protagonist and the audience that the latter could have its fear and pity tempered by the pleasure of seeing an action imitated. The playwrights of our own time who handle equally volatile materials have adapted many of the same ritualistic elements for their plays; the reduction of dialogue to ritual or its parody in Beckett, Pinter, Ionesco, and others;

the nonrealistic acting styles of many absurdist plays—all have as their purpose setting distance between audience and play. The poets who handle the most dangerous materials are also most concerned with poetic form. Anne Sexton says:

> I used to describe it this way, that if you used form it was like letting a lot of wild animals out in the arena, but enclosing them in a cage, and you could let some extraordinary animals out if you had the right cage, and that cage would be form. [8]

Anne Sexton employs a great variety of thematic and technical shapers on her poetry, so many, in fact, that it might be more accurate to criticize her unsuccessful poems for having too much rather than too little form. Thematically her poems are often built around such paired contrasts as guilt and love, truth and falsehood, mobility and fixity, illness and health. Other themes develop incrementally from poem to poem: the double image, the mirror and the portrait—all used to speak of the past and present confronting each other, the conflicts of parent and child, or the testing of identity by measuring it against family history; sin, guilt, belief, grace, and love worked through a number of poems about Christ or traditional Christian faith; the connection of writing to finding health.

One preoccupation in her poetry which acts as an informing principle for both theme and technique is ritual. This preoccupation expresses itself in her use of words or images commonly associated with rituals—"sacrament," "ceremony," "rites," "ritual," "magic," "exorcise," "communion." These, and words with similar connotations, occur frequently in enough of the poems to indicate at the very least a kind of compulsive pattern by which the poet tries to make sense of what she is saying. Similar effects come from poems built on the rhythms of children's rhymes which, as M. L. Rosenthal says, "catch the note of the self reduced to almost infantile regress."[9] These patterns provide a framework in which irrational acts can be understood or order imposed on chaos.

More important in the poetry, however, is the making of rituals, or the discovery of ritual meaning in an ordinary action. Without claiming to exhaust or fully distinguish all the rituals in Anne Sexton's poetry, we may speak of three kinds which predominate: rites of *mastery*, in

8. Marx, "Interview with Anne Sexton," p. 568.
9. Rosenthal, *The New Poets,* p. 134.

which power is tested or exorcised; rites of *initiation* or *cleansing*, in which the poet looks for confirmation of a new insight or stage of growth, or experiences testing, purification, or absolution; and rites of *communion*, where some gesture or order of words opens up a sense of oneness with others.

"You, Dr. Martin," the first poem in her first book, is about power, but this subject is explored by acting out rites of mastery. The poem is addressed to a therapist under whose power the hospital inmates stand. He represents order, "God of our block, prince of all the foxes." The inmates "stand in broken lines," awaiting "the shibboleth" which will open the gates and let them go to dinner, where they "chew in rows." The images emphasize the helplessness and childishness of the patients and the false connections of words and ideas which characterize madness—"the frozen gates of dinner," "we move to gravy in our smock of smiles." But they also illustrate the meaninglessness of this order; the rows and broken lines lead to nothing, the order is for its own sake. Because it demands helplessness and childishness, the poet perceives this order as judgment. The doctor has a "third eye," a magical way to see into lives; it is "an oracular eye in our nest." Dr. Martin symbolizes power. In his name the shibboleth is pronounced, the intercom calls; his eye is the oracle which both sees and speaks. And the poet responds "of course, I love you"—an act of submission and abnegation.

Another power is present in the poem, however, and it is also evoked in ritual terms. This is the power of submission and childishness: the unraveled hands, the foxy children who fall. The poet asserts herself as "queen of this summer hotel" and even "queen of all my sins/forgotten." The power has no channel or focus yet, "we are magic talking to itself," but it is more genuine and capable of meaning than the perfect order imposed by the hospital. "Once I was beautiful. Now I am myself," and it is from that standpoint that she asserts her power in the rituals she makes out of naming and counting.

"We are magic talking to itself" introduces a connection between therapy and making poetry. In "Said the Poet to the Analyst," the poet says, "My business is words. . . . Your business is watching my words." Where the analyst wants to make words refer to facts or events so he can determine whether they correspond to the truth, the poet speaks of words as "like swarming bees," alive and vital, creating their own shape. They do not tell the truth, they control it; they are ritual or magic.

THE SACRAMENT OF CONFESSION

In "The Black Art" the theme is repeated. The events of life are never enough, either as experience or as meaning.

> A woman who writes feels too much,
> those traces and portents!
> . . .
> A man who writes knows too much,
> such spells and fetiches!

The poem is not concerned primarily with distinguishing women from men or feeling from knowing; instead, it separates these ways of entering and valuing experience—each conceived of as magical—from the trivial data of experience itself. A writer is a spy or a crook, one who discovers or steals secrets, in the poem. He is also a perverter of order for the sake of nature. "With used furniture he makes a tree."

"You, Dr. Martin" is concerned with two kinds of power—the power of the therapist-parent who imposes a mechanical order on the patient, and the power of the patient-child, who discovers a deeper order or a more meaningful disorder through madness and poetry. Many of the other poems explore other kinds of power and sources of order. Sometimes our perception of the triviality of order comes through a poem's rhythm. "Ringing the Bells" develops like the final verse of "The House that Jack Built," in one long run-on sentence where no event or impression is subordinate to any other. Neither causality nor chronology matters as a means of explanation; "and" or "who" introduce each new element in the poem to operate at the same dead level.

> And this is the way they ring
> the bells in Bedlam
> and this is the bell-lady
> who comes each Tuesday morning
> to give us a music lesson....

Patients, attendants, and music therapist become automatons, revealed by the childlike telling of the verse, which continues in one sentence for twenty-eight and a half lines, until the whole illusion of meaningful pattern and activity is demolished in the last lines of the poem:

> and although we are no better for it,
> they tell you to go. And you do.

Settling family estates and disposing of the remains of history provide the narrative peg for several of Anne Sexton's poems. Here putting things in order becomes a weighty ritual action which issues in either an exorcism or a benediction. In some of the poems, the poet expresses her love simply by retracing the steps of a relative or ancestor. "Tonight I will learn to love you twice," she says in "Some Foreign Letters," addressing the old maid aunt whose letters reveal her secret sins and desires. In "Walking in Paris" she reenacts the youthful past of the old aunt, measuring herself against that other life as though she were the old woman's twin:

> You are my history (that stealer of children)
> and I have entered you.

In "Funnel" she makes yet another ceremony of meeting the ancestors, in this case celebrating the richness and openness of the past, the mouth of the funnel.

> I sort his odd books and wonder his once alive
> words and scratch out my marginal notes
> and finger my accounts.

Sorting becomes the chief ritual of mastery in these poems. "Funnel," "All My Pretty Ones," "Elizabeth Gone," "Division of Parts" begin or end with the act of sorting and arranging the relics of the past. From this imposed, perhaps arbitrary, order, remembering, forgiving, and releasing can follow.

"All My Pretty Ones," generated and sustained by old documents and photographs, becomes a meditation on inheritance—on how to "disencumber" the dead father and the living child from past failures. Sorting means putting proper value on the past and knowing what may be discarded, and what must be kept "to love and look at later." The father's nature—"my drunkard, my navigator/my first lost keeper"— must be affirmed, and so the poet keeps a three-year diary which documents the father's alcoholism, for

> Only in this hoarded span will love persevere.
> Whether you are pretty or not, I outlive you,
> bend down my strange face to yours and forgive you.

Discarding the past does not disencumber us. Moving back through one's history means painfully untying each of its knots all over again, forgiving one's past and the actors in it. On the surface, *sorting* is simply the method anyone uses for making the judgment whether to keep or discard, but as it becomes the process by which the poet relives the past, celebrates times, places and people, and arrives at conclusions, it takes on some of the characteristics of *sortilege*, omen-reading or casting lots, a word to which it is etymologically close.

For M. L. Rosenthal the successful confessional poem must achieve a fusion of "the private and the culturally symbolic," and be more highly charged than other poems.[10] One strategy for achieving such a fusion is to turn private idiosyncratic gestures into formal rituals or to play the private rite off against the public one.

An exceptionally rich poem which brings together ordering, exorcising, and the traditional patterns of Christian observance is "The Division of Parts," where things which are simultaneously "debts," "obstacles," and "gifts I did not choose," must be sorted. Against that action proceeds the observance of Good Friday and the anticipation of Easter, in which a similar working out of debts and unchosen gifts occurs on the public level. *Dividing* is a key to the poem: making the distinctions which separate gifts from debts and performing the acts which turn debts into gifts are the acts which disencumber the past and allow the poet to claim her real inheritance. Two kinds of inheritances are at issue, the effects left by the dead mother—money, "letters, family silver,/eyeglasses and shoes,"—and the complex of attitudes, emotions, doubts, and guilts with which children must also come to terms as their heritage. In this poem that second kind of inheritance is symbolized by "The clutter of worship" taught the poet by the mother, of which she says:

> I imitate
> a memory of belief
> that I do not own.

The poet must come to terms with both her mother and with Christ, and in both cases this means asserting her adulthood in defiance. Defiance causes guilt, but it also opens the way for genuine grieving. Or, to put it in the terms established through the rituals in the poem, the mother, described variously as "sweet witch," "worried guide," and "brave ghost," must first be exorcised before she can be invoked. The

10. Ibid., p. 80.

poet must "shed my daughterhood," an image sustained by a series of references to inherited clothes, the coats, stones, and furs which "settle on me like a debt." The same cluster of images establishes an identity between Christ and the mother.

> And Christ still waits. I have tried
> to exorcise the memory of each event
> and remain still, a mixed child,
> heavy with cloths of you.

In an earlier stanza the poet has identified the mother and Christ in images recalling the crucifixion—the thieves and the casting of lots for Jesus' garments—but also establishing the complex relationship between guilt and grief.

> I have cast my lot
> and am one third thief
> of you. Time, that rearranger
> of estates, equips
> me with your garments, but not with grief.

Daughterhood, the heavy cloths, the clutter of worship must all be shed until they can be "owned," both acknowledged and possessed. The poet must reject the "dangerous angels" who call on her to convert and the tempting image of Christ, on whom so many have "hitched" in trouble, and find another way which is her own. It is not the way of conversion but the way of deprivation, imaged by Jesus, the "ragged son" of Easter. Her way, tentative and incomplete even when the poem is finished, is suggested by the exorcism-invocation of the last stanzas. The poet has a dream while wearing her mother's nightgown, a dream which reenacts the struggle for mastery which is at the heart of the poem and the particular ritual patterns which shape it. What greater power can there be than the power over spirits which characterizes Jesus in the Gospel of Mark? The mother, "divided," climbs into the daughter's head, only to be cursed and expelled, *Dame/keep out of my slumber./My good Dame, you are dead."* Recalling this at noon on Good Friday, the beginning of Christ's agony on the cross, the poet sums up her ambivalence by speaking of both cursing and summoning her mother through her "rhyming words." And indeed, the entire next to last stanza in Part IV of the poem is made up of epithets by which the mother is invoked, celebrated, and finally laid to rest. The grief, which would not come when the poet "planned to suffer," because it was blocked by guilt, flows now into the phrases of invocation and benediction:

> my Lady of my first words,
> this is the division of the ways.

The conjunction of the dream and the hours of sorrow commemorating the crucifixion recalls the journey to the underworld to meet the parents which is so often found in ancient myth and epic. The hero goes to meet the past, calls up his parents to learn about the future, and then returns to the world in which he is about to meet his most important adventures. Surely it is not strained ingenuity to see the same psychological pattern being worked out in "The Division of Parts," the ritual acting out of the passing of power from parent to child. The child asserts maturity, now, by taking an independent course. And, because the relationship with Christ has also been one of childlike dependence, or a temptation to "convert" to another's expectations, He too must be taken leave of, so that the poet can come into the real inheritance from Him. Therefore the last stanza of the poem shows us Christ fastened to His crucifix, still the ragged son and sacrifice, not the triumphant Lord who might demand obedience. The poet identifies with the tormented man, not with a theology of sin and salvation which might keep her a child. Christ remains on the cross "so that love may praise/ his sacrifice/ and not the grotesque metaphor." And as Christ has no power over her, neither has the mother, now only a "brave ghost" who *fixes* in the poet's mind, incapable of giving or withholding "praise/or paradise," but by that very incapacity setting the poet free to enter and affirm her real inheritance.

What we have called rituals of mastery occur elsewhere in the poems. Typically, they shape either the poet's response to the guilts of the past or to the making of poetry as a way of imposing order on life. In "A Story for Rose," for example, the poet controls memory and fear of death on an airplane ride by making a story of them. In "Mother and Jack and the Rain," the tensions of the poem revolve around the "haunting" and "cursing" of the rain outside and the "affirming" of the room and the "endorsing" of the poet's womanhood by her memories; but the tensions are resolved by the making of poetry, by the poet's "conjuring" her daily bread. The thematic and formal significances of rituals of mastery come together:

THE INNER WAR

With this pen I take in hand my selves
and with these dead disciples I will grapple.
Though rain curses the window
let the poem be made.

Whereas the rites of mastery tend to dramatize conflicts with the God-like authority figures of doctors and parents, those of initiation and cleansing tend to dramatize the poet's role as mother to her children, or to be concerned with moving from shame for the body to affirmation of it. Such a statement of the case is too schematic to be true, of course, but it separates out a tendency in the poetry which rewards close examination.

Houses, rooms, cells, caves, and other images indicating close confinement symbolize the body, especially in the volumes *All My Pretty Ones* and *Live or Die*, as though the self were an unwelcome inhabitant in a hostile environment. "Housewife" develops this pattern of imagery most clearly, opening with the assertion "Some women marry houses./ It's another kind of skin . . . ," and closing with "A woman *is* her mother./That's the main thing." Here two equivalences, woman equals house, and woman equals her mother, establish the sense of entrapment against which the rituals of cleansing or initiation work, for their effect is to help the poet find escapes from the trap for herself or her daughters. In "Those Times" the poet describes a "bedtime ritual," "nightly humiliations" when she was "spread out daily/and examined for flaws," at the age of six. She describes her body as "the suspect/in its grotesque house," locked all day in her room, behind a gate. In defense against a mother who keeps her a prisoner to prevent divorce, the poet withdraws even further, withholding herself from the mother's breasts, from the well-made dolls, retreating into the closet, "where I rehearsed my life." Rehearsing fantasies becomes planning growth into womanhood "as one choreographs a dance"; meanwhile, she acts out another kind of fantasy, "stuffing my heart into a shoe box." The poem exploits images of testing and probing, especially through the bedtime ritual on the bathroom tiles, to express guilt and shame for being female. There is no cleansing or release here, though the poet looks forward to the time of maturity, when "blood would bloom in me/each month like an exotic flower . . ." and children "would break from between my legs. . . ." The poem, though it speaks of rituals, and shows us a child making ceremonies to protect herself, does not lead us to a resolution in those terms. Instead, menstruation and parturition become the adult counterparts of or fulfillments of the shameful rituals.

"Those Times" can serve as a gloss for other poems where the ceremonies are efficacious. "The Lost Ingredient" is one such poem. It deals with many kinds of loss—the lostness of the past, of the salt sea which was our beginning, of "rites," and of the "ingredient." The word "lost" appears six times in the twenty-four line poem, all but once at the end of a line, and is echoed in the near-rhymes "last," "loosed," and "lust" which close four other lines. "Steal" or "stole" and its near-rhymes end seven more lines. These two key words, "lost" and "steal," shape not only its rhyme but also the poem's thematic development. The gentle ladies in Atlantic City bathe in salt water to gain "impossible loves," "new skin," or "another child," but they sit in bathtubs, "smelling the stale/harbor of a lost ocean." In the second stanza the poet swims in the Salt Lake, "to wash away some slight/need for Maine's coast," and to "honor and assault" the Salt Lake "in its proof." As the gentle ladies of the first stanza wished to recapture lost rites, the poet makes her own washing an evocation of something she calls "proof," some confirmation of the self. She goes on to associate this with Reno, where she also performs the ceremonies of gambling for the sake of a "better proof." This evidence, or lost ingredient, must be wrested from life, from time, from the salt sea; the rite becomes the way into this evidence, a gamble to "keep us calm and prove us whole at last." But in the poem the ingredient stays lost, not even identified in its absence; all we know is that salt, money, or lust have no power to uncover it. The poet has made a ritual action out of ordinary events, and we are aware of the enormous organization and control which informs the poem, but the reader remains aware only of loss and mystery.

Initiation into being a woman, which the poet calls being twice-born, controls the action of the poem "Little Girl, My String Bean, My Lovely Woman." The child, poised on her twelfth year, inhabits a body which is about to be possessed by the new powers of fullness and ripeness. The poet speaks of the daughter's body as a "home" or "place" about to be entered by the ghost hour, noon, when the sun is at its zenith. The images work together to hint at magic and mysterious powers, a divine possession of the soon-to-be-fruitful girl, but the poem also associates this new becoming with the original birth, when the child was "a world of its own/a delicate place." The change in the body does not come from outside, however, but from within; even so, it must be greeted with an act of initiation, and on that account the girl is described as separated from her body, needing to let it into her self:

> Oh, darling, let your body in,
> let it tie you in,
> in comfort.

To be initiated is to learn some new truth by having it acted out before or with one. So it is here; the body's changes are confirmed and celebrated—"there is nothing in your body that lies./All that is new is telling the truth." Initiation rites often have to do with possessing something; and here too the poem provides confirmation. The daughter is not an alien in the house of her body; at the end of the poem she possesses it, and the poet urges her to "stand still at your door,/sure of yourself, a white stone, a good stone." Let the noon hour in, let the sun in, let the body in, let newness and the truth in, then stand at the door, in possession of the house: so the ritual of initiation goes in the poem.

Perhaps the best example of the ritual of cleansing and initiation—and a fine poem—is "Pain for a Daughter." The title itself suggests some of the meanings working in the poem—the daughter's pain, the poet's pain on behalf of the daughter. The poem grows out of the contrast between blindness in several metaphorical senses and seeing or knowing. The daughter is described variously at the beginning of each stanza as blind with love, then with loss, pain, and fear. As she moves through these feelings, from love to fear, she loses her mastery over situations in return for knowledge. In the first stanza, blind for love of horses, she overcomes her squeamishness to treat her pony's distemper, draining the boil and "scouring" it with hydrogen peroxide. In this case her love makes her blind to the distastefulness of the job and lends her a capacity she did not have. "Blind with loss," she asserts her mastery over the neighbor's horses, but is injured and returns home, hurt and frightened. Here her father performs "the rites of the cleansing" on her injured foot, cleaning it with hydrogen peroxide, and, for the first time, her eyes are mentioned: "eyes glancing off me," "eyes locked/on the ceiling, eyes of a stranger." Though the eyes do not see, they are an index to her *knowing* in the face of her pain. She cries to God for help, where a child would have both cried to and believed in her mother. The rites of cleansing have introduced her into the adult world, symbolized not by a cry of hope but by one of despair. Her seeing parallels her mother's, who sees her daughter's life stretched out, her body torn in childbirth:

> and I saw her, at that moment,
> in her own death and I knew that she
> knew.

Anne Sexton speaks of writing as putting things in place, having an ordering effect on her own life. "I mean, things are more chaotic, and if I can write a poem, I come into order again, and the world is again a little more sensible and real. I'm more in touch with things." It is not surprising, seeing how the poems work, that Anne Sexton thinks of form as a kind of magic for discovering the truth.

> I'm hunting for the truth. It might be a kind of poetic truth, and not just a factual one, because behind everything that happens to you, every act, there is another truth, a secret life. [11]

Nowhere do we see her commitment to the discovery of the secret life behind things more clearly than in those poems, many of them dealing directly with the figure of Jesus or the traditions of Christianity, built around rites of communion, prayer, and gift-giving. These poems are her most complex work, for they do not simply rest on traditional forms of words and actions to counterpoint or frame the struggle for peace or unity, they explore a profound ambivalence about the Christian understanding of life. Christianity, in the full force of its explanation of human existence, entices her, as the epigraph from Guardini in *All My Pretty Ones* indicates: "I want no pallid humanitarianism—if Christ be not God, I want none of him; I will hack my way through existence alone. . . ." The prayers or acts of communion in the poems, then, are neither ironic parodies nor secularized ceremonies; they are, rather, expressions of the deepest human needs in the full consciousness that "need is not quite belief."

"With Mercy for the Greedy" illustrates the point. It is addressed to a friend who has urged the poet to ask a priest for the sacrament of confession and has sent her a cross to wear. The poet prays, not to the cross, but to its shadow, detesting her sins and trying to believe in the

11. Marx, "Interview with Anne Sexton," p. 563.

cross. But what draws her is the crucified man—"I touch its tender hips, its dark jawed face,/its solid neck, its brown sleep"—just as in "The Division of Parts" she affirms the sacrifice and not "the grotesque metaphor." The cross around her neck taps like a child's heart, "tapping secondhand, softly waiting to be born," but it cannot come alive for the poet precisely because it represents so complete and final an answer. As Yeats resolves the debate between Soul and Heart in the Heart's favor—"What theme had Homer but original sin?"—Anne Sexton chooses the sacrament of poetry over the sacrament of confession. Or rather, she chooses the particular kind of sacrament of confession which poetry is, its kind of mercy, its wrestle with words and meanings.

We cannot know whether prayer, confession, or communion would lack efficacy for the poet; we only know that she cannot permit herself to yield to them. When they occur, they are magic incantations or childish pleas for a miracle, as in "The Operation."

> Skull flat, here in my harness,
> thick with shock, I call mother
> to help myself, call toe of frog,
> that woolly bat, that tongue of dog;
> call God help and all the rest.

Here is an implied answer to the pious believers who brag that there are no atheists in the trenches; one will believe or try anything, if only the fear is great enough, but it will be in shame at the reversion to such immaturity. In "Letter Written on a Ferry While Crossing Long Island Sound," the poet pleads for a comic miracle, that God should let four nuns break loose from the pull of gravity and float through the air, doing "the old fashioned side stroke," and then she imagines it happening, with the four nuns crying out *"good news, good news,"* as well they might.

"For the Year of the Insane" is subtitled "a prayer," and addressed to Mary, but order and form are fragmented; "There are no words here except the half-learned,/the *Hail Mary* and the *full of grace*." The beads lie *unblessed*, and hammer in on her like waves as she counts them, for the poet knows herself an unbeliever. The words and beads associated with the worship of Mary do not convey a sense of grace but of further condemnation, as the poet moves further into silence and madness. The fragmented prayer gives way to an equally fragmented holy communion, where the bread and the wine also become images of damnation;

the wine burns, and the poet says "I have been cut in two." Mary does not respond, the bread and the wine do not change, no communion occurs. The prayer for grace, for "this crossing over" is denied, and the poet remains "in the domain of silence."

Communion occurs both between man and God and between man and man; and the efficacious ritual symbolizes and facilitates both kinds of communion. It is not accidental or arbitrary that such rituals include eating and drinking. They represent what Philip Wheelwright calls "assimilative ritual," which he says "consists in reaffirming and attempting to intensify man's continuity and partial oneness with nature, or with the mysterious creative force behind nature." [12]

The hunger for communion is the hunger for assimilation, oneness with others, and with what Anne Sexton has called a "secret life" behind things, and for self-transcendence, getting out of oneself and "in touch with things." In "For the Year of the Insane," no one but the poet appears; she is handed wine, and she invokes Mary, but the prayer for self-transcendence only confirms her isolation.

> O little mother,
> I am in my own mind.
> I am locked in the wrong house.

"Hunger" is a ruling word in *Live or Die*. In "Flee on Your Donkey" and "Suicide Note" the same line appears, "O my hunger! My hunger!" The former poem describes madness as a kind of hunger, and the poet finally turns, not to answers to save her, but to her hungers, exhorting them to turn and "For once make a deliberate decision." In "Suicide Note" we are told that "Once upon a time/My hunger was for Jesus," but again there was no fulfillment. Roman Catholic theology speaks of taking communion in a state of sin as eating and drinking damnation, precisely what "For the Year of the Insane" commemorates. So does "Wanting to Die," where a suicide attempt becomes a kind of black mass, a perverted communion service aimed at overcoming the enemy, who is both life and death.

> Twice I have so simply declared myself,
> have possessed the enemy, eaten the enemy,
> have taken on his craft, his magic.

12. Philip Wheelwright, *The Burning Fountain* (Bloomington, Ind.: Indiana University Press, 1954), p. 179.

THE INNER WAR

The hunger for death in Anne Sexton's poems is equally a hunger for meaningful life, for choice, and for affirmation. Being hungry need not mean there has been no communion, only that it was not enough for the speaker's appetite; so she can say of the suicide attempt, "To thrust all that life under your tongue!—/That, all by itself, becomes a passion." "The Addict" further elaborates images of communion to speak of the lure of suicide. The pills are "a mother," "loaves," and "a diet from death," but they also keep the speaker in practice for another attempt to die. This addiction to "goodnights" is "a kind of a marriage/. . . . a kind of war"; it is a ceremony and a sport, filled with rules, and taking the pills demands

> . . . a certain order as in
> the laying on of hands
> or the black sacrament.

All these images work to suggest the complexity of the hungers to be met by this communion service, for the ritual brings together the best and worst relations human beings have with one another—war and marriage—and tries to make sense within those limits. The poet takes the pills and lies on her altar, "elevated by the eight chemical kisses." No consecration occurs on this altar, however, just as no love or affection come with the chemical kisses. We know what the poet wants, what the ceremony tries to evoke, only by their absence: self-acceptance, "I like them more than I like me," maturity, "I'm a little buttercup in my yellow nightie," and a sense of love and sacramental order. The final lines are a child's jingle, mocking the longings which shape the poem.

A suicide attempt means taking one's life in one's own hands, being responsible for it; this addiction parodies suicide and gives up responsibility for one's life. In many of her poems Anne Sexton tries to impose order on events by inventing ceremonies or insisting that something is a rite, that a bed or a stretch of beach is an altar, that irrational gestures or forms of words could hold off events, as in "Lament," or gain forgiveness, as in "Christmas Eve." Rituals, like symbols, grow out of their own inner principles, however; we cannot invent meaningful rituals, we can only discover them. In Anne Sexton's poetry there are a great many rituals which do not work *as ritual*, though many of them help the poems work.

THE SACRAMENT OF CONFESSION

That distinction may seem forced and arbitrary, since poetry has always been close to, when not a form of, magic, and the connection between prophet, priest, and poet is as real as it is ancient; nevertheless, distinguishing the effects of ritual, especially that rooted in traditional Christianity, from those of the poetry which supports or grows out of it, in Anne Sexton's poetry, is essential. For of the three kinds of rituals discussed here, those which most closely depended on traditional Christian imagery and gestures were also those in which the meaning of the poems was most widely separated from the meaning of the rituals. What I have called rituals of mastery, where the poet struggled for ascendency over the God-like doctor, the authoritarian parent, or the chaos of past history, succeeded in and through the poems, on the two levels demanded by Rosenthal, the personal and the culturally symbolic.

Poems which employed ritual language to speak of cleansing, initiation, prayer, or communion often succeeded in being culturally symbolic precisely to the extent that they revealed an isolation and anxiety on a personal level which was not to be relieved by rituals. The poet's intense attraction to Jesus, the man who suffers for others, and Mary, the perfect and all-forgiving mother, always stands at odds with the worship which attends both those figures. Anne Sexton's poetry chronicles a struggle to come of age: to work through the conflicts with the parents in order to forgive and be forgiven; to break free from the guilts and inadequacies of the past and become open to others; to become the kind of parent who sets her children free and thus breaks the cycle of guilt and shame which has marked her family history. If we are to believe some theologians, the need of our time is also to come of age, to set aside the comforts of cult and ceremony and live affirmatively in a totally secular world. "Need is not quite belief," Anne Sexton has said, and that is a kind of gloss on our times. So is the description of Protestants she puts in an eight-year-old's mouth in "Protestant Easter":

> Those are the people that sing
> When they aren't quite
> sure.

A. R. Jones says of Anne Sexton's poetry that "her framework of reference is ultimately religious,"[13] that is, that the values she insists

---

13. A. R. Jones, "Necessity and Freedom: The Poetry of Robert Lowell, Sylvia Plath and Anne Sexton," *Critical Quarterly* 7 (1965): 25.

on are traditional religious ones. The argument of this chapter is that her poetry is largely shaped by attempts to enlarge a traditional Christian framework which has been a chief source of the psychological suffering she has endured. It would be a mistake to say that she is working her way out of that framework, since the same issues, questions, and answers have a way of recurring over and over in a lifetime, and her first play, *Mercy Street*, takes place during a celebration of Holy Communion, but the evidence of *Live or Die* and *Love Poems* supports the opinion that the poetry has worked its way to a new level of apprehension of that framework. *Live or Die* closes significantly with the poem 'Live,' which gathers up most of the major themes and preoccupations of her previous work and looks ahead to the affirmations of her last book, *Love Poems*. Surveying the course of her life, as it has been charted in the book, the poet acknowledges how things have been distorted by her "dwarf-heart's doodle," and how turned inward and entrapped she has been. The attempts to tell the truth became lies; the body was naked, even when she dressed it up. Now she asks a question whose answer implies a judgment on her strategies for making sense of things, especially the psychological, social, and personal rituals she has invented, "Is life something you play?"

Now, however, life opens up within her; the sun, which has been an important image in a number of the earlier poems, where it has gone from being a threat to being benign, now shines from within, purifying her. This inward change is confirmed by the love of her family, who replace her ceremonies and rituals with games and playfulness.

> If I'm on fire they dance around it
> and cook marshmallows.
> And if I'm ice
> they simply skate on me
> in little ballet costumes.

Love Poems by its very title leads us to expect a change from the earlier books of poetry, and the poems bespeak the self-acceptance toward which "Live" has moved. Even unhappy love and the sorrow of being the other woman exist in the context of hope. Truth and the secret life do not now come through obscure or tortured rituals; things are their own meanings—the pleasures of physical love, delight in the human body, trust in the lover, pain and anger at loss. Whereas many earlier poems seemed to impose meaning by insisting on the sacralization of things, the ceremonies of *Love Poems* are all playful, desacralized, celebrating the simply human. A ritual completes some kind of action and confirms its meaning by referring to the secret life underlying ordinary life. Making, constructing, building, harvesting, all of them key terms in *Love Poems*, are ordinary human occupations; they complete actions, too, but according to a plan or blueprint. When these terms become metaphors for lovemaking, they take us into a new way of creating ceremonies. "But your hands found me like an architect." "I am alive when your fingers are." "Oh, my carpenter,/the fingers are rebuilt." "He is building a city, a city of flesh."

In her work so far, Anne Sexton has penetrated deeply into chaos and has tried a number of strategies for working her way through it. In some of these strategies therapy and poetry have come together; confession has brought relief by putting things in order in the process of sharing the shame and suffering; the devices which protect the reader from too much reality also protect the writer. And if these ways of handling her material have narrowed the range of her themes, that may be a necessary price to pay for the depths she has reached. If, as seems to be the case, the poetry *has* been therapy, and the fever chart now points toward greater health, a major index of this—and perhaps something of a cause as well—is the movement from the tight confinement which rituals of mastery, initiation, and communion are attempts to break to the playful games of lovemaking which characterize Anne Sexton's last book of poems.

It is no disparagement of those earlier poems to say that *Love Poems* shows more health than the previous three books, since without them no such change can be imagined. They are the record of spiritual struggles which have issued, however tentatively and provisionally, in new degrees of self-acceptance and affirmation of love and human communion. They are also testimonies to the power of poetic forms to give point and substance to spiritual struggles. As Anne Sexton says, in speaking of what constitutes the truth in her poetry, "The effort is to try to get to some form of integrity when you write a poem, some whole life lived, to try to present it now, to give the impact." [14]

14. Marx, "Interview with Anne Sexton," p. 564.

3

The Live World

If Robert Bly's magazine, *The Sixties*, has an editorial policy, it is to probe the American psyche, to diagnose its ills and offer means for it to become healthy. Whole issues of the magazine are put together as coordinated assaults on the evils of American culture. In critical articles and by precept and example in the poetry it publishes, and especially in the foreign poets whose works it translates, *The Sixties* opposes the egocentricity, formalism, sensationalism, and subservience to dead traditions which its editors see as characterizing modern American writing. Often the magazine connects these failures of the psyche with the larger evils of American society—our involvement in Vietnam, the ugliness of urban life, our misuse of nature. It is the purest consistency which has led Robert Bly to cancel the subscriptions to his magazine of universities which have taken government defense contracts. The argument is frequently farfetched; Bly acknowledges that refusing his magazine to the university library makes no impact on the huge institutes and centers which are supported by defense contracts, but he sees a connection between the failure of our imagination in art and the failure of our moral imagination in the way we act as a nation. And for Bly, particularly, the making of a poem is a moral act, an opening up to new depths in the self, deeper than the ego, from which not only words and images but acts must arise. "All expression of hidden feelings involves opposition to the existing order."

How these preoccupations articulate throughout Bly's work is richly exemplified in the eighth number of *The Sixties* (Spring 1966). The entire issue, which contains translations of nineteenth century German poetry, Bly's review of Lowell's *For the Union Dead*, and a long review of James Wright's poetry, takes coherent form around Bly's introduction to the translations, "The Dead World and the Live World." In this essay, Bly distinguishes two kinds of writers, those who bring us "news of the human mind" and those who bring us "news of the universe." The first produce poetry locked in the ego, while the poetry of the second "reaches out in waves over everything that is alive."

American literature, he argues, is dominated by those who study the human faculties of feeling, will, and intellect as though the human being existed without reference to the rest of existence. "Writers of this kind regard the 'I' as something independent, isolated, entire in itself, and they throw themselves into studying its turns and impulses." The culture which produces literature which never studies the human in relation to the non-human or even in relation to lives in other countries, he argues, "will bomb foreign populations very easily, since it has no sense of anything real beyond its own ego." And the poets, no matter how critical of or alienated from their culture—and surely the vast majority of the writers Bly is criticizing share with him their opposition to the Vietnam War and the social evils which it has come to represent—who give us only "news of the human mind" can only take refuge in the sensational and extreme. "Poets of the sort," he says, referring specifically to the confessional poets, "will accept calmly the extinction of the passenger pigeon or the blue whale."

That is the dead world, the world of the merely human, which, to remain interesting, must be exaggerated and inflated. It is a world without genuine interiority, for Bly. Poems made from the stuff of that world will necessarily deal with the inflation of the ego, with the kind of excessive self-consciousness which Dostoievsky called a disease, with the suffering of alienation from others. The live world, on the other hand, is aware of an additional energy beyond the human energies of feeling, will, and intellect. This energy within the self Bly follows Georg Groddeck in calling the *Gott-natur*, which he translates as the "holy-nature."

> The *Gott-natur* senses the interdependence of all things alive, and longs to bring them all inside a work of art. The work of these poets is an elaborate expression of the *Gott-natur*. What results is a calmness.[1]

1. Robert Bly, "The Dead World and the Live World," *The Sixties*, no. 8 (Spring 1966): 3.

He calls for a poetry which goes deep into the human being, "much deeper than the ego, and at the same time is aware of many other beings," which is aware of human nature as a part of nature, and he cites the poetry of Gary Snyder, and Japanese and Chinese poetry as examples of awareness of *Gott-natur.*

The implications of Bly's essay are wide-reaching. To sketch in just a few of the most obvious, the poet of the universe would know both the inner and the outer world as one; he would therefore be a political rebel in his society even if he would not call himself alienated from it; he could not let his nation bomb foreign populations *or* exterminate the passenger pigeon. In his attack on James Dickey's *Buckdancer's Choice,* he says if the anguish of the poems were real, "We would feel terrible remorse as we read, we would stop what we are doing, we would break the television set with an ax, we would throw ourselves on the ground sobbing."[2]

The poetry of the universe should differ from that of others as much in form as in theme. While it tried to bring the whole live world within a poem, the result should be calmness, not the extravagance or self-generated excitement of a Ginsburg or Kerouac. And indeed sparsity, rather than long catalogues of things, characterizes the poetry Bly admires and writes himself. And though critics speak of "subjectivism" when talking about Bly's poetry, he cites with approval Groddeck's claim that Goethe's short poems are impersonal, as though "not created by a person but by nature." The deeply subjective poem, one which reaches the deepest parts of the self, should somehow become impersonal. Emotions would not be suppressed, but excitement over one's experiences or feelings would be channeled and diffused into this universe of which one was a part. The reading of oneself into the world, so typical of the romantic's attempt to overcome the subject-object dichotomy, would not be inappropriate so much as useless as a poetic strategy.

Further light on the poetic forms which might come from this new consciousness of the inner world comes from the article on the poetry of James Wright which appears in the same number of *The Sixties.* The essay is signed "Crunk," the usual signature for the longer critical pieces

2. Robert Bly, "The Collapse of James Dickey," *The Sixties*, no. 9 (Spring 1967): 74.

in the magazine, but the views and sentiments are consistent enough with Bly's that guessing at authorship seems unnecessary.

The essay, which reviews Wright's work from *The Green Wall* (1957) through *The Branch Will Not Break* (1963), takes on in battle virtually the whole American literary establishment to argue that Wright has freed himself from what Crunk sees as the typical American concern for discursive reasoning, tight metrical from, moral and philosophical truisms in poetry. The world of such a poem is, of course, the dead world Bly speaks of; Crunk makes Kenyon College at the height of the Ransom years his symbol for it. Writing a poem meant climbing out of the world into a walled-in garden with tame animals for decoration. "When people praised order in a poem, as they did much in those days, they were praising the ordered world possible to them only in a poem." Crunk's argument is not with order or form, however, so long as the poem can exploit its form to give us inklings of the terror, ferocity, and wildness which exist in the world. "It is the world which has these things in their full force. The work of art shows their tails escaping under the door, and we know by this that they are in the next room."[3]

When the new critics and the poets they arose to explicate spoke of poetry as existing in and of itself, without reference to the world of experience, they were fighting a rearguard action against science and empiricism. When even so sensitive a reader as I. A. Richards could try to save poetry by justifying it as composed of pseudo-statements for the sake of organizing emotions, and so eminent a practitioner as T. S. Eliot was content to speak of poetry as merely a higher form of amusement, the battle was desperate. Poets and critics retreated behind walls like medieval monks, trying to preserve something from the barbarians. Those who climbed the other way, out of the poem as a world "in little," an independent, self-contained "mode of existence," were also those Bly excoriates in his review of *For the Union Dead*, the *Partisan Review* writers, "the alienated establishment intellectual" concerned with the interaction of politics and art.

To go out where the wildness is means to open oneself to guilt, paranoia, self-hatred; to reach through that wildness, in the self and the world, to the calmness Bly speaks of, calls for new ways of making poetry—new models, new expectations, new ways to employ language. Crunk tells us that, after reading Georg Trakl's poetry in 1952–53,

3. Crunk, "The Work of James Wright," *The Sixties,* no. 8 (Spring 1966): 52–78.

James Wright concluded that his own work was not poetry. "It had not helped anyone else to solitude, and had not helped him toward solitude."

On the basis of these two essays in this remarkable issue of *The Sixties*, it is possible to trace out what Robert Bly expects from poetry, what its materials are, and how it should be written. Crunk attacks the critics of Wright's poetry who want "meanings" and "relationships" established by logic and association, arguing that such discursive writing simply goes over already familiar intellectual and psychological ground. Putting "thought" and "meanings" in poetry means simply being able to handle moral platitudes; establishing "relationships" through association means staying within the bounds of those areas of consciousness already mapped, "areas like the old Canadian wilderness that has now become 'rationalized'." Poetry, for Bly, should bring us "news of the universe," and Crunk reminds us that the poet who gets far enough in himself, back into the unmapped regions of the brain, will bring back "some bad news about himself, some anguish that discursive reasoning had for a long time protected him against." Poetry should bring to consciousness what is hidden, not merely from the ego, but from those depths in which we are aware of kinship with the universe. Somehow anguish, bad news, self-hatred, paranoia—all of them necessary consequences of this penetration to deeper levels of consciousness—must be transformed, through the energy of the image, into goodwill toward the self, calmness, and solitude.

When we turn to the poems in Bly's first book, *Silence in the Snowy Fields* (1962), we see how he exemplifies the principles he enunciates in his criticism. What is chiefly significant about the book is not its themes but the forms in which they are developed. In a prefatory statement on his work, Bly speaks of the connection between poetry and simplicity and points out that the structure of the poems is simple—many of them are made up of three parts, with a time lapse between them, and "If there is any poetry in the poems, it is in the white spaces between the stanzas." Winter landscapes occur frequently; darkness, dryness, blankness characterize many of the scenes the poet reflects upon, and loneliness and death are thematic preoccupations. But none of this strikes us as threat or deprivation. Landscape and theme are somehow affirmative, taken into the realm of silence so that we may reflect on them with a kind of detached enjoyment.

We are rarely surprised by anything in Bly's poems; even the tricks of perception are deliberately kept on the surface, rendered most often through similes so that we are kept aware that one thing is not being forcibly *made into* another by a human mind. The mind plays with resemblances for its own enlightenment, but the things themselves keep their own identity. At the same time, because there is no insistence on something *made* by the poet, and we believe that we see connections only because the poet does, we accept that "One thing is also another."

> The darkness drifts down like snow on picked cornfields
> In Wisconsin: and on these black trees
> Scattered, one by one,
> Through the winter fields—
> We see stiff weeds and brownish stubble,
> And white snow left now only in the wheeltracks of the
>   combine.
>
> ("Three Kinds of Pleasures")

The stanza contains four simple adjectives, one unobtrusive simile, two verbs in the active present tense, neither of them very kinetic in effect, and three other verbals. These provide all the *action*, if that is the right word for it, in the stanza. What we have is description which, except for one simile, uses language almost purely *denotatively* or *presentationally*. But the effect is far greater than cataloguing parts of speech can suggest, for the very impersonality of the scene and its independence of an observer, work on the reader, and "we see" becomes the pivot on which everything turns. We become aware not merely of the starkness of black trees scattered among winter fields, but of the play of black and white implied by the simile and repeated by the image of white snow in the wheeltracks. We are used to snow drifting down on dark fields, as we are used to dark wheeltracks through snow; reverse the images and we become aware of the interpenetration of white and black, light and darkness. It is like looking at the Chinese ideograph for nothingness, *mu*, executed in a thick, black flowing image against a stark white surface; one knows that the image *means* emptiness, nothingness, the incomprehensible. It denotes what cannot be denoted. All our ordinary experience leads us to imagine nothingness as like the blank white paper, but that blankness has been violated by another ordinary way of expressing the concept, the written word. The play of black and white, background and foreground, image and imagination, what the eye sees and what the mind's eye conceives, takes us beyond ordinary experience as we contemplate the ideograph. Such an interpenetration of objects and images, where "one thing is also another" while remaining truly itself, characterizes Bly's most effective poetry.

It is not arbitrary association which leads a reader to think of Zen calligraphy of Chinese ideographs in connection with Bly's poetry. The haiku of Japan and the drinking song of fourth century China provide rich models for what he wants to do. His admiration for the lyric poetry of the six dynasties runs through both his criticism and his poetry. In the poetry it not only appears thematically, in such a poem as "Chrysanthemums," dedicated to Tao Yüan-ming, it exerts a profound influence on the form. Flatness of statement, ellipsis, simple metaphors and similes, juxtaposing of images so that a scene and the emotion it evokes flow together, characterize the style of his models. Through this style they reflect the inwardness which is so important to Bly.

The poet in such poetry is not a *maker* who imposes shape upon existence or creates a verbal world to retreat to, but neither is he a *seer* or visionary, as those terms have been used to speak of symbolist or surrealist poetry. For the *seer*, who twists and falsifies ordinary experience for the sake of extracting its inner meaning, frequently succeeds only in freeing locked-up areas of his own psyche. Dreams, fantasies, verbal play, freudian wit, the worlds of unreality and madness typify theme and method for the *seer*. And Bly has some harsh words to say for such poems, which become "like a tank, unable to maneuver on soft ground."

> How strange to think of giving up all ambition!
> Suddenly I see with such clear eyes
> The white flake of snow
> That has just fallen in the horse's mane!

This poem, "Watering the Horse," can serve as an example of how the oriental simplicity of his poetry reveals the inner world. Like a haiku, it does not lead us through the steps of a meditation, but distills the meditation into its conclusion and confirms it by the clarity of image which follows upon it. The notion of giving up ambition, letting go of this world, takes the poet by surprise. Thought produces a feeling: "how strange." Once again, the pivot of the poem is the simple verb, "I see," and once again it carries us into the life of things. Clear sight follows insight; thought, emotion, sight become a single experience, an enlightenment, anchored in the vivid perception of a white flake of snow in a horse's mane.

To speak at such length of a twenty-eight word poem may seem a sad example of breaking a butterfly on the wheel, but perhaps this butterfly is strong enough to survive. In any case, "Watering the Horse" is a good test case for deciding whether one wants to read any more of Bly, for it shows in miniature his strengths and weaknesses. Not every reader will be persuaded of the depth of excitement signaled by two exclamation points in four lines. The poem's terms are so narrow that even the most willing reader may find that he cannot enter the inner world of the poem without some more detailed confirmation of the experience. Even the longer poems in *Silence in the Snowy Fields* will frustrate or please in exactly the same way, however. Scenes are rendered presentationally, as they make their immediate impact on the senses. Vivid images seem to be deliberately suppressed; the verb "to be" predominates, as though the poet's chief purpose is to affirm the simple existence of what he sees. In "Driving Toward the Lac Qui Parle River," some form of "to be" appears five times in the first six-line stanza, always working as a copula to link each sense impression or experience with the rest. Nothing stands subordinate to anything else, because these are not ideas to be linked into an argument but physical images to convey what the poet means by "I am happy."

> I am driving; it is dusk; Minnesota.
> The stubble field catches the last growth of sun.
> The soybeans are breathing on all sides.
> Old men are sitting before their houses on carseats
> In the small towns. I am happy,
> The moon rising above the turkey sheds.

The language and imagery are deliberately flat, but as we look more closely at the buried metaphor in "The stubble field *catches* the last growth of sun," called to our attention only by the turn of phrase in the second half of the line, details lift up from their context. Dead or inanimate things live; the stubble field catches, the sun grows, the soybeans breathe. The old men sitting before their houses and the soybeans breathing partake of the same quiet vitality. In many of Bly's poems, animate and inanimate objects change places or lend their natures to one another, with the effect of stressing liveliness, not deadness. Thus the rising of the moon, a kind of accompaniment to the poet's happiness, becomes a sign of vitality like the sun's growth.

The poet enters this scene in "the small world of the car" which "Plunges through the deep fields of night." For a moment the reader is aware of the worlds represented in the poem, the larger world of living, breathing things and the closed independent world of the car which passes through it. But the car is also a "solitude covered with iron," an image for a peculiarly contemporary hermit's hut, a place of retreat to solitude. "Inner" and "outer" are unhelpful terms for describing these worlds, however, for they commit us to subject-object, good-bad dichotomies despite our best intentions.

These two worlds do not stand over against each other as opponents in a dualistic universe, for, whatever happens in the poetry of *The Light Around the Body* (1967), his second book, Bly does not intend to speak dualistically. He therefore takes what would be a stock image for the evils of industrialism—Detroit and all its works—puts it in a setting which would be a stock image for the simple life, and reverses their usual connotations. The car plunging into the deep fields of night becomes the inner world of man penetrating into the deepness of nature, and nature in turn plunges into the "solitude covered with iron," for the car is "penetrated by the noise of crickets." This last image achieves much the same effect as a famous haiku by Basho, "The Stillness":

> So still:
>> into rocks it pierces—
>> the locust-shrill. [4]

Just as in Basho's poem stillness and the high-pitched sound of the locust blend natures, become one, and are then capable of piercing into the hardness of rocks, so the insubstantiality of the crickets' sound penetrates the hardness of iron. The two worlds interpenetrate and become one; "inner" and "outer" cannot distinguish their natures, for each borrows attributes from the other. Nothing has a fixed nature, nothing is good or bad; we perceive the holy-nature's energy running through the man-made world of the car as well as through the silent fields and the noise of crickets.

The final stanza of the poem extends this development. "Water kneeling in the moonlight" and lamplight which "falls on all fours in

4. Harold Henderson, *An Introduction to Haiku* (Garden City, N.Y.: Doubleday Anchor Books, 1958), p. 40.

the grass" effect the same kind of interpenetration. The water comes to life in the natural light, while the man-made light comes to life as it falls on the grass. When the poet reaches the river, where for the first time other people enter the poem, the rising moon which was the signature for his happiness in the opening stanza is now full and at its height, covering the river. The poet reaches his destination, physically and spiritually—a flowing river bathed in moonlight, on which a few people in a boat are talking low. The world of nature and the world of men, of human conversation and natural beauty, are one. All the details of the poem, the reversals of expectations, the exchanges of attributes and images of interpenetration, work together to substantiate the phrase "I am happy."

Speaking of Georg Trakl's influence on James Wright's poetry, Crunk says, "In Trakl a series of images makes a series of events." The same may be said of the best of Bly's poetry. Often we are aware of the events as a series of correspondences between the outward scene and the buried life within the poet. So in "Hunting Pheasants in a Cornfield," the poet asks, "What is so strange about a tree alone in an open field?" and arrives at his answer by describing the scene and discovering that the mind is like the tree, "It stands apart with small creatures near its roots." In "Night" he perceives the same kind of interplay between surface and depth, the high and the subterranean. The box elders are full of joy "Obeying what is beneath them," the butterfly carries loam on his wings, the toad bits of gravel in his skin, as though they too had sprung from the earth itself. Everything lies asleep, obeying the night and what is beneath them, gaining vitality from their chthonic origin. The correspondences are not always explicit or detailed—indeed they could not be without degenerating into the kind of moralistic platitudes inveighed against in *The Sixties*—but in the best poems the reader feels acted on by this hidden life to which the images point. In "Where We Must Look for Help," for example, Bly substitutes the Babylonian account of the flood for the Genesis story, so that the sign of hope does not come with the dove of peace but the "spider-colored crow." The Noah story is gone; what remains is the dove who found no resting place, the swallows who always return home, and the ugly crow—which in Genesis is the first to leave the ark but in this poem flies on the third day. The poem divests these images of any symbolic quality they might have gotten from the original tale. They operate on us, therefore, not as symbols of peace or flight, but as simple, even despised, fellow-creatures. The image of hope and help is ugly, tough, a scavenger.

> The crow, the crow, the spider-colored crow,
> The crow shall find new mud to walk upon.

Silence in the Snowy Fields organizes its poems around the epigraph from Jacob Boehme, "We are all asleep in the outward man." The book is divided into three parts, "Eleven Poems of Solitude," "Awakening," and "Silence on the Roads." While it would be hard to argue that each poem belongs exactly where it is within this arrangement, the groupings themselves tell us something important about the aim of the whole book. The poems of solitude are, for the most part, quiet meditations anchored in and tested by the stark landscape of late fall and winter in the upper midwest of America. Inner and outer cohere and interpenetrate, and the poet speaks of joy and happiness. Solitude brings one kind of awakening, a cleansed perception of the unity of things.

"Awakening," the second section of the poems, touches more directly upon death, sorrow, division between the two worlds. Thom Gunn, arguing that the differentiating human consciousness has not come into Bly's world yet and that it is "a world of total innocence, without evil, and simply for enjoyment," has not sufficiently considered this section of the book. "Unrest," "Awakening," "Depression," and "A Man Writes to a Part of Himself" speak ominously of the dark world. They also demonstrate the burden it places on Bly's imagination when he must deal with the two worlds in opposition. In "A Man Writes to a Part of Himself," the speaker writes as though to his wife, whom he imagines starving, exposed to the elements, hiding in a cave. He describes himself "On the streets of a distant city, laughing, With many appointments," though returning at night to sleep in a bare hotel room, "a room of poverty." The poem is simple and touching; the separation within the self, conveyed by simple contrasts between cave and bare room, sorrow and artificial gaiety, husband and wife, engages our sympathies. At the same time, we recognize that the poem rests on the stereotype of the traveling salesman or businessman away from home. If we could imagine Willy Loman having enough inner life to write a poem, this would be what we would expect. The final lines of the poem put the question:

> Which of us two then is worse off?
> And how did this separation come about?

But only the extreme simplicity of the poem saves it from the effect of the stereotype. It is too easy to see the businessman as representing the dead world completely cut off from the live world represented by a stereotyped feminine nature.

"Silence on the Roads," the final section of the book, contains poems which seem most clearly to represent the clarity of sight which comes when the outward man finally awakes, when he has experienced both the healing of solitude and the unrest and depression of knowing the world of spiritual darkness.

> We know the road; as the moonlight
> Lifts everything, so in a night like this
> The road goes on ahead, it is all clear.

In Bly's first book, there is little of what Thom Gunn and other critics want when they speak of "thought" in poetry. Indeed, Bly's whole program repudiates any such content as valid for the creations of the new imagination. While it is not accurate to say, as Gunn and others have argued, that the world of these poems is prelapsarian, it is true that there are few human beings in the poetry and "it is only by other human beings and their acts that his view of the world can be tested." With *The Light Around the Body* that issue rises in compelling fashion. If the first book had little "argument"—because showing the inner world required little—the second book takes its shape from the argument that we live in two worlds which do not meet as one. Inwardness can be excessively private, and we may need more evidence to be persuaded of the happiness or joy the poet announces than the cluster of images in the poem provides. In *Silence in the Snowy Fields* we are often willing to suspend rational judgment and take the statements as given. In *The Light Around the Body* Bly wants to persuade us, but the poetry does not testify to the coherence of inner and outer world, it criticizes the turmoil and falseness of the latter from the standpoint of a longing for inwardness. When other people enter this poetry, they are intruders and destroyers.

The influence of Boehme, at least as represented by the epigraphs introducing four out of five sections of the book, has increased. The first section, "The Two Worlds," is introduced by a passage which speaks of our being generated out of both the inward and the outward worlds and needing therefore to speak and be understood in two languages. The passage offers no hope that these two languages can be translated into one another or that they are equally capable of telling the truth. In fact, as the passage puts it, "according to the outward man, we are in this world, and according to the inward man, we are in the inward world. . . ." The quotation from Boehme which introduces the second section, "The Various Arts of Poverty and Cruelty," makes the point more explicitly: we have been locked up and led blindfolded by the wise of this world, who have done so with their *art* and rationality, "so that we have had to see with their eyes." "We have been captured by the spirit of the outward world . . . and now death has us," Bly quotes Boehme in the fourth section, "In Praise of Grief."

"Monistic systems develop in ages of comparative tranquility, dualistic and pluralistic systems in ages of doubt and transition. Boehme was dualistic, his attention was fixed both on the sensual and the supersensual."[5] Certainly Robert Bly is a powerful witness to the turmoil of this age and demands of poetry that it describe the inward changes which grow out of the profound changes in the outward world in our time.

> There is an imagination which realizes the sudden new change in the life of humanity, of which the Nazi camps, the terror of modern wars, the santification of the viciousness of advertising, the turning of everyone into workers, the profundity of associations, is all a part, and the relationships unexplained. . . . There is an imagination which assembles the three kingdoms within one poem: the dark figures of politics, the world of streetcars, and the ocean world. [6]

In *The Light Around the Body* the two worlds are those of the damned and the saved, the evil and the virtuous. The interpenetration between the two worlds for the enrichment of each, which was an important influence in the earlier poetry, rarely occurs in the second book. In "The Two Worlds," for example, the representatives of the outward world are Romans, executives, merchants, accountants, President Johnson's cabinet. They are not ignorant of the inner world; they are its enemies. The conflict between the two worlds is a death-struggle. The inner world is identified with solitude, sorrow, love, and especially with the mother. In "Romans Angry About the Inner World," the

---

5. Howard H. Brinton, *The Mystic Will* (New York: Macmillan, 1930), p. 8.
6. Robert Bly, "Five Decades of Modern American Poetry," *The Fifties* 1 (1958): 38–39.

Romans seize Drusia, whose crime is that she has "seen our mother/In the other world," and torture her to death, for "The two Romans had put their trust/In the outer world." Romans, executioners, and executives appear in the poem, as though any term would readily substitute for the other. The other world terrifies them; it is "like a thorn/In the ear of a tiny beast!"

"Smothered by the World," "A Dream of Suffocation," and "Watching Television" speak of the horror of this world, where machines and men become interchangeable and "Accountants hover over the earth like helicopters." The events of this world and the consequences of its history are so inimical to the inner world that, as the poet watches television, the body cells "bay" and "the inner streets fill with a chorus of barks." Finally

> The filaments of the soul slowly separate:
> The spirit breaks, a puff of dust floats up,
> Like a house in Nebraska that suddenly explodes.

The poet does not lead us to observe or enter a scene from the calm center of a unified life; we accompany an angry prophet, savagely parodying and condemning the false religion he sees. "The Busy Man Speaks" illustrates the point. The Busy Man intones a two-part creed, first renouncing the faith he will not follow, then affirming his allegiance to the other. He renounces the mother of solitude, of art, of love, of human and physical nature, of Christ. He will give himself only to the father, the foundation for what might be called the religion of outward man, the worship of business, cheerfulness, righteousness, and the practice of the Protestant virtues.

> From the Chase National Bank
> An arm of flame has come, and I am drawn
> To the desert, to the parched places, to the landscape of zeros;
> And I shall give myself away to the father of righteousness,
> The stones of cheerfulness, the steel of money, the father of
> rocks.

In his criticism, Bly has been preoccupied with defining the new imagination which will explore the unknown country, the "change in inward life which corresponds to the recent changes in outward life." When he catalogues those changes, however—and the list always includes industrialism, modern advertising, concentration camps, and rarely much that is hopeful—we are forced to conclude that his own earlier poetry does not show us *correspondences* but *compensations* or *alternatives* to the changes in outward life. His midwestern landscapes are made timeless by being made historyless, or the history is innocent because naive and unselfconscious. "Some day I will go back, and inhabit again/The sleepy ground where Harding was born."

History has entered the world of *The Light Around the Body*, and timelessness means only that the sins of the past are eternally present, or, as Bly puts it in the title of one poem, "After the Industrial Revolution, All Things Happen at Once. ' The blank landscape of the midwest now becomes a palimpsest on which every generation has written its bloody crimes. And we have a vision, in Aldous Huxley's words, of time apprehended as one damned thing after another. Bly telescopes time to bring the Hessians at Trenton, the Whiskey Boys, Coxey's army together as one army, Henry Cabot Lodge, Henry Ford, Charles Wilson together as a single lying sloganeer. Similarly, "As the Asian War Begins" describes Conestoga wagons filled with murderers crossing the Platte River, in "Hatred of Men With Black Hair" those who praise Tshombe and the Portuguese in Angola are those who skinned Little Crow and overthrew Chief Joseph, and in "At a March Against the Vietnam War" the poet sees the darkness the Puritans brushed as they went out to kill turkeys.

> Underneath all the cement of the Pentagon
> There is a drop of Indian blood preserved in snow:
> Preserved from a trail of blood that once led away
> From the stockade, over the snow, the trail now lost.

This stanza sums up American history; the Pentagon, a symbol for irrational, evil power to people who share Bly's political views, stands like an altar over the sacralizing drop of blood, the saint's relic from which it takes its strength. The religion is the worship of power—of business, righteousness, and stones—"We make war/Like a man anointing himself." In "Hearing Men Shout at Night on Macdougal Street," the poet translates the present noise into the sounds of the first New England slave-ships setting out. Politicians—Andrew Jackson, Theodore Roosevelt, John F. Kennedy, Lyndon Johnson, Dean Rusk—become devil-figures in the poetry, and American history becomes demonolatry. Apocalyptic provides the tone—"The world will soon break up into small colonies of the saved,"—but the apocalypticism does not rest in a promise of deliverance but only in a conviction that we must atone for the evil being done. The American self-hatred Crunk spoke of in James Wright's poetry permeates Bly's work in *The Light Around the Body*. The energy and promise of human evolution become perverted into "The Great Society," where man is unnaturally cultivated to change places with the machinery he created to serve him. Evolution and history seemed to have a direction and goal, but they have been lost or perverted: "Hands developed with terrible labor by apes/Hang from the sleeves of evangelists." In "The Fire of Despair Has Been Our Saviour," Bly reflects on the course of human history since the Ice Age, the tracks leading out of the snowbound valley of that life. Those tracks have been lost, even as the trail of blood from the stockade was lost and only one drop of Indian blood remains enshrined under the Pentagon.

> This autumn, I
> Cannot find the road
> That way: the things that we must grasp,
> The signs, are gone, . . .

The Light Around the Body is a despairing book. The solitude Bly invited in his earlier works has given way to isolation; the natural world which he celebrated and through which he saw a spiritual, inner world, the correspondences instinct with value and significance, have gone, and only a pale compensation for the outer world gleams through. The poetry does not speak of hope but only of an apocalyptic day of wrath in which atonement might occur. Bly keeps faith in an inner world, but it stands in judgment on this life rather than infusing it with moral energy.

> . . . where has the road gone? All
> Trace lost, like a ship sinking,
> Where what is left and what goes down both bring despair.
> Not finding the road, we are slowly pulled down.

Since the publication of *The Light Around the Body* Bly has published two small booklets of poetry, *The Morning Glory* (1969), twelve prose poems, and *The Teeth-Mother Naked at Last* (1970), a seven-part antiwar poem. He has also edited an anthology of political poetry, *Forty Poems Touching on Recent American History* (1970), to which he has contributed a superb preface called "Leaping Up Into Political Poetry," and has continued to publish new poems and translations in various magazines. The recent poetry has come out of a time of testing, an apparent exile from the peace of the inner world. It shows the marks of a hard transition, but it also evidences new power, particularly in the political poetry. This is especially noteworthy, since it was the political poetry of *The Light Around the Body* which was most severely criticized by the critics. Even a friendly critic, Richard Calhoun, said of the political poetry:

> My objection is not to the content but to the poems as poetry. His lines are too often trite, flat, unimaginative—merely rhetorical. . . . There is very little of the sanction of poetry in these poems, even in the pity, which is self pity, and especially in the anger. The poet here has a truth to speak rather than a nightmare to imagine for his reader.[7]

"Writing Again," published in the *Tennessee Poetry Journal*, testifies to the struggle with his material which Bly has gone through.

> Oval
> faces crowding to the window!
> I turn away,
> disturbed—
>
> When I write of moral things,
> the clouds boil
> blackly!
> By day's end
> a room of restless people,
> lifting and putting down things.
>
> Well that is how I have spent this day.
> And what good will it do me in the grave?

On first reading, the poem seems to commemorate a failure, a return to writing which does not eventuate in the kind of poem the poet wants. Disturbance, the threat of storm, and finally a room full of imagined people who move things out of their places: these are at the farthest remove from the silence and solitude out of which the poet had wanted his earlier poems to grow. And the last two lines remind us of the realization which led James Wright to change his approach to poetry: "It had not helped anyone else to solitude, and had not helped him toward solitude."

7. Richard Calhoun, "On Robert Bly's Protest Poetry," *Tennessee Poetry Journal* (Winter 1969).

Yet, as the poem continues to work on us, the final lines speak not of despair but of calm strength. The whole poem then becomes the account of the poet's opening himself to turbulence, turning away from the cheap grace of isolation from others. He may have spent the day in frustration as a poet, but he has kept faith with the moral issues he faces. We could not believe what he writes about moral issues if the clouds did not boil blackly and the room fill with restless people. Only because he has spent the day well, in moral activity, can he ask his final question, which points beyond this day to an examination of the whole life. The poem is a success, describing a failure. It leads us to the right question—What has my work to do with ultimate things?—and leaves the answer open.

In a prefatory note to *The Morning Glory*, Bly speaks of recognizing how independent of us an animal is. "Its world is complete without us. We feel separated at first; later, joyful." The prose poems themselves do not penetrate into that world which is complete without us, however. They read like rough notes from a poet's journal, sketching in external appearances and making a few tentative essays at comparisons which will turn these alien scenes or objects into something from our world. In "A Small Bird's Nest Made of White Reed Fiber," the similes which connect the object with the poet's experience stress disjunction. The simple instinctual architecture of the bird's nest reminds the poet of cloudy transoms over Victorian doors and the tangled hair of nurses in the Crimea. The comparisons convey a sense of deprivation—deprivation of light, of sleep, of love. The nest, made and forgotten, is compared to "our own lives that we will entirely forget in the grave." It is white, but we will be reborn black.

The independence of this world seems to judge the poet. Addressing a dead wren, he says, "Forgive the hours spent listening to radios, and the words of gratitude I did not say to teachers." Elsewhere he says, "There is something spiritual in the rocks with their backs turned to me." A dry thistle shouts at his sleeping senses, "called in from the back of my head," but it speaks of loss, "some love we forget every day." The bottom plate of a turtle's shell is "like the underside of some alien spaceship." Sea imagery occurs frequently in the prose poems, but its effect is to convince us that we are not amphibians, able to move in two worlds. We are land-bound.

The prose poem is at home in French, where writers have been able to employ rhythmic prose and heightened emotion in description to create something neither traditional poetry nor ordinary description or anecdote. But the prose poem has always been an anomaly in English. Following the French model, it becomes a purple patch; refusing to do so, it tends toward flaccidity. Our deepest acquaintance with the form is likely to be in religious tales or parables. The successful prose poem in English depends on resonances set up in the reader's mind which do not rest primarily on pronounced rhythm or especially elaborate metaphorical structure. It is likely to be anchored either in description of nature or in a narrative. One might cite passages from Faulkner, Thomas Wolfe, and James Agee to exemplify the kind of writing where recollection of the past is evoked through such a vibrant poetic prose. Thoreau in *Walden* and in his journals frequently writes a subtler, less mannered kind of nature description with the resonances the effective prose poem must have.

Bly's prose poems lack both emotional intensity and vigor of language. The special difficulties of the form therefore stand out clearly. The poems stand outside what they describe. We are more aware of the observer than of what he observes, and what we perceive is how important it is to him that what he sees should possess deeper meanings. So he experiments with idiosyncratic, peculiar comparisons whose effect is not to join scene and observer's mind but to stress how thoroughly disjoint they are. The poems are diffuse rather than concentrated. The comparisons lack either the inevitability of shared perception or the surprise of vivid insight. The similes are strained; they convey opinions rather than insights. We become aware of the simile as a rhetorical device rather than as a way of seeing.

If there are two stages to our relation to a world which will never be our friend, separation and joy, these poems come from that first stage, no matter how much the poet wants to speak of joy. Their form describes opacity, a closed and indifferent world where rocks turn their backs on us and we ask forgiveness of dead wrens for the failures of our lives.

Yeats says we make rhetoric out of our quarrel with others but poetry out of our quarrel with ourselves. Too often in *The Light Around the Body* we are aware of rhetoric, a sign of judgment from outside the world of the Romans and executives. In his preface to

Forty Poems Bly speaks of the need to "leap up" into political poetry, first by diving down deep into one's own psyche, then by springing into the national psyche. The poet must leave his own concerns for a time and live in that other realm. When he returns, he brings strange, alien forms of life, "which he then tries to keep alive with his own psychic body." That means writing out of love rather than hatred, showing a care to be identified with the opponent rather than an anxiety to stand separate from him.

Bly calls for a language which "entangles" the personal and the divine, which draws together political life and personal growth into one fabric. The language must be "fragrant"; it must be redolent with the life people know. Such language in a political poem will not be used to express opinions or recommend an action; it will "entangle" poet and reader in a common life—the life of their society and of the universe. Many of the war poems in *The Light Around the Body* are by these standards unsuccessful. But, by these same standards, *The Teeth-Mother Naked at Last* is a fresh, powerful, and profoundly successful work.

The Teeth-Mother brings the political and personal and cosmic together into one long poem. By turns stately and flat, bitter, sorrowful, satiric, and prophetic, the poem works in a multiplicity of tones. We hear the voices of public officials, interrogators of prisoners and soldiers spliced into the extravagant language of surrealism and the equally extravagant, though different, language of satire. Perhaps the nearest analogue for the poem's shape is the greater irregular ode which the romantics developed for speaking simultaneously of several levels of experience. Coleridge's anguished political ode, "Recantation," most closely compares with Bly's poem.

The poem opens with a description of planes and helicopters taking off on missions in Vietnam, an orderly, even beautiful activity which is immediately set in two contexts, the historical and the natural. "This is Hamilton's triumph," an inevitable result toward which American history has always pointed. It has the inevitability too of a natural catastrophe, an event heralding the change of seasons. "This happens when the leaves begin to drop from the trees too early. . . ." Placing the war in these two time-schemes, the historical and the seasonal, gives us an essentially biblical view of it. As the prophets saw the Assyrians and Babylonians as simultaneously heaping guilt on themselves by their evil

51

actions while inescapably working out the will of God, so Bly sees American might as evil in its expression but essentially a helpless agent of power and energy it cannot comprehend. That power is natural and moral in its effect—the change of seasons, the icing over of lake water which drives life deep to the bottom, if it is to survive. By contrast, "Supersabres/like knots of neurotic energy sweep/around and return." The image conveys the whole contrast. American power is knotted, neurotic, turning on itself. It is energy without a proper end.

But the war is not allegorized away. Artillery shells explode, napalm bursts into flame, children and rooms explode, "800 steel pellets fly through the vegetable walls." An American sergeant is also dying, realizing as he does that "the mansions of the dead are empty, he has an empty place/inside him. . . ."

Part II builds on this biblical foundation by placing affirmations of belief in the trinity and on building democratic institutions in Vietnam in ironic juxtaposition against the screams of a tortured prisoner. The President's rallying cry turns into the whines of jets which "pierce like a long needle."

> As soon as the President finishes his press conference,
>   black wings carry off the words,
>   bits of flesh still clinging to them.

Ministers, professors, television, and priests are all liars. Their lies set out "like enormous trains of Conestoga wagons. . . ./And a long desire for death flows out, guiding/the enormous caravans from beneath." Again the imagery reminds us of the two contexts of history and nature.

The dying soldier was born with an emptiness he used half his skin to cover. The leaders desire "to take death inside" for the thrill of feeling something. Later on, Part IV describes a fast-revolving black silo within our own bodies, with motorcycles rearing around on the silo's inside walls. The lies become like those knots of neurotic energy, and the President's press conference a chain of nervous tics symptomatic of deep ill. He lies about when the Appalachian Mountains rose, the population of Chicago, the composition of the amniotic fluid, "And the Attorney General lies about the time the sun sets." Emptiness and lies—the signs of a desire to die which has us in thrall. "Do not be angry at the President. . . ./He is drifting sideways toward the dusty places."

Asserting that our lies mean we want to die calls for some causal explanation. In Part III historical cause-and-effect becomes explicitly moral in its working out: "That's what it's like for a rich country to make a war."

> It's because the aluminum window-shade business is
>   doing so well in the United States that we roll fire
>   over entire villages
> It's because the milk trains coming into New Jersey hit
>   the right switches every day that the best Vietnamese
>   men are cut in two by American bullets that follow
>   each other like freight cars.

The causal connections cannot hold logically, but the associations built up by linking milk trains and bullets following like freight cars, window shades and rolling fire create emotional and psychological connectives which do persuade us. Our economic system becomes another grid through which power follows its own volition. Caught in the grip of our economic system, we are its agents and its beneficiaries alike: "That is what it's like to have a gross national product." We are insulated from suffering by our wishes and therefore do not even imagine we have victims.

Essentially the first half of the poem has been organized as a study of power: first the harnessing of energy symbolized in planes and ships; then the energy of the will which turns that other energy into the power of bombing and strafing; finally a comparison of human and mechanical power with cosmic power. The power to kill is like the power to lie; starting out as an assertion of the will to destroy another, it becomes instead an act of self-destruction. A moral causality operates, even through the absolute and amoral laws of economics. *We want to die because we have everything else* would sum up the argument thus far.

Anger and grief break through these sections, but the handling has been almost impersonal, the tone appropriate to describing implacable and unharnessed forces.

The second half of the poem, four shorter sections, is intensely personal. First person pronouns predominate; the emphasis shifts to how *we* feel. "We all feel like tires being run down roads under heavy cars." The black silo revolves inside our own bodies; the New Testaments are fleeing from us. Our emptiness and helplessness spring from sinful pride. Power intoxicates:

> The Marines think that unless they die the rivers will
> not move.
> They are dying so that mountain shadows can fall north
> in the afternoon,
> so that the beetle can move along the ground near the
> fallen twigs.

Judgment and pity have been delicately balanced in the poem. Our indignation at lies has been tempered by pity for the liars; our anger at the savagery of soldiers has been modified by our sorrow for the triviality of their deaths. But in Part VI the poet tests those sometimes contradictory emotions against the vision of a burning child walking toward us. Judgment, pity, indignation, and sorrows are civilized feelings. Before the savage reality of this napalmed child, however,

> I would suddenly go back to my animal brain;
> I would drop on all fours, screaming,
> My vocal chords would turn blue, yours would too,
> It would be two days before I could play with my own
> children again.

The poem has ranged widely, but it comes back to a single clear focus in the image of the burning child and in the utterly primitive, and deeply humane, response of the scream. The final section of the poem is generated by that image. Exhaustion, the end of struggle, the yielding up to natural power open Part VII. At first this seems to be escape. "I want to sleep awhile in the rays of the sun slanting/over the snow." It is not escape, however, but an opening up to another power, symbolized by the dust shaken from the daffodil and the particles of Babylonian thought passing through the earthworm. The wind working above the earth dispersing pollen and the earthworm working beneath it, refreshing the soil by working the remains of ancient history into it, serve cosmic time. There are ends toward which the world moves by evolution or catastrophe. We can work with these ends or try to oppose them with our own, but the result will be the same. The poem now gathers up the earlier images of natural force, particularly the image of the ice beginning to show its teeth in ponds. Motion speeds up, rushing toward catastrophe; pigs rush over the cliff, like the Gadarene swine. The waters part and huge spheres come to the surface, not bubbles of decay but images of judgment. The luminous globes contain "hairy and ecstatic rock musicians," symbols of a new society, a counter-culture, everything terrifying about the future to a dead generation. And in the ocean is "the teeth-mother, naked at last." The image of the mother appears frequently in Bly's poetry, but nowhere with more terrifying effect than here. In "The Busy Man Speaks," the speaker repudiates all ties to the mother and gives himself away to the father of rocks and righteousness. The mother—protective, nurturing, identified with nature's benevolence—now shows the other aspect of these qualities: savage in defending her children, inexorable in judgment. Divine power uses the Babylonians and the Americans as its instruments, then discards them. It is the Old Testament vision, expressed in surrealistic images.

The poem's final words call for withdrawal and return, withdrawal to the inner world of nature and return as outcasts

> crouched inside the drop of sweat
> that falls again and again
> from the chin of the Protestant tied in the fire.

Only through separation, even at the risk of encapsulation, and identification with the martyrs, can we escape death by freezing, the judgment of offended nature, the teeth-mother.

The poetry which successfully took us into the inner world, and transformed the outer world in the process, exploited images rooted in landscapes and natural settings. It dealt with the present, as Bly says in his prefatory statement in *Silence in the Snowy Fields*. Now the subject matter has broadened out, and Bly deals with history, politics, human guilt, and society's corruptions. To ask that such themes lead to the kind of placidity and quiet joy which marks the earlier poetry would be to ask that Robert Bly become Pollyanna. We must be grateful when any poet tries to tell the truth about such subjects. He has brought the three kingdoms of politics, the streetcar, and the ocean into one poem, but the result is not what he had anticipated in the earlier poetry. To bring these three together and still make one's goal the kind of imagery which leads us into the inner world where we celebrated the holy-nature, will lead to a retreat into sentimentality or despair. Howard Brinton, writing of the circular process by which Jacob Boehme reconciles the inner and outer beings, says:

> In every completed act of the will the soul goes from earth through hell to highest heaven and back to earth again. This is the dialectic of all organic life. Boehme's universe is dramatic to the core, for everywhere the two wills endeavor to enact their ap-

pointed roles. Sometimes they fail and the darkness of evil over-shadows them. When they succeed, the light of heaven shines. [8]

What Howard Brinton says of Boehme reads like a gloss on Bly's poetry. In *The Light Around the Body*, the darkness of evil overshadows the holy-nature Bly wishes to discover throughout the universe. The vision becomes a Gnostic one, as it must when devil-figures enter a dualistic system. The American self-hatred becomes projected onto history, politics, other men. Though Bly says we must atone, the means of atonement, the possibility of human redemption have not yet entered the poetry thematically; the inner world is as closed to Dean Rusk, Lyndon Johnson, and the Romans and business executives as the Garden of Eden. But surely the apprehension of the holy-nature working in the universe means one must believe that we are all to be saved, whatever that means, or none. In *The Light Around the Body*, the only savior Bly holds out to us is "The Fire of Despair." His pursuit of the inner world image had taken him deeply into things, but not deeply enough to overcome the distinctions between the two worlds.

The Teeth-Mother has both scope and depth. It breaks free almost totally from the hatred, fear, and demonology which weighted down the war poems of *The Light Around the Body*. It is not free from the excesses of political rhetoric, but Bly has plunged into his own psyche and found it like his nation's. He bears his guilt and can therefore speak in both the traditional prophetic voices—the call to judgment and the more tender call to turn and repent.

8. Brinton, *The Mystic Will,* p. 23.

4

That Scarred Truth
of Wretchedness

In 1971 James Wright published his *Collected Poems*, his fifth book of poetry. The first bore the imprimatur of W. H. Auden, testifying that it was an example of what might be called *classical modern* American poetry. Both *The Green Wall* (1957) and *Saint Judas* (1959), his second book, showed two tendencies at work, often in opposition to one another. On the one hand there was the kind of subject Wright wanted to handle, the dream-world, death, ghostly visitation, the chaotic life of whores, murderers, and fugitives; on the other was the poetic form, the shapes in which he wanted to mold his subjects. The poetry displayed that control one expects from traditional modern poetry: the power of a sensitive spirit disciplined by a firm intellect and a craftsman's skill.

Organization is the hallmark of his early work; traditional forms and traditional stances characterize the poems. Epigraphs introduce the books and sometimes individual poems as well, throwing light, creating interesting ambiguities, setting up tensions. The epigraphs help organize our responses, as do the section headings, titles, and frequently tight metrical patterns. Laments, elegies, and a morning hymn appear in *The Green Wall*. Both "To a Fugitive," about a man escaping from the police, and "Saint Judas" are in sonnet form, though the subject in each case might easily have repaid more expansive treatment.

Some of the works, particularly "Crucifixion on Thursday," "The Angel," and "Come Forth," depend for a measure of their effect on the reader's recognizing a parallel with biblical themes. Though these have vitality and interest, they also carry some of the burden of all such reworkings, a tendency to sound like conscious updating rather than a fresh discovery of the poetic possibilities of an old story.

One is always aware of two things in these first two books, a strong current of feeling and intense absorption in the lives of the characters Wright observes, and a great variety of poetic devices, ways of providing sufficient detachment from what he is writing that the poet can mute his feelings, dilute passion into what critics like to call "compassion."

"Morning Hymn to a Dark Girl" praises a black prostitute in the kind of high-flown language which makes her a subject for poetry by obscuring everything about her as a person. She becomes an occasion for metaphors, an object for the poet's mind to muse on: "Summoned to desolation by the dawn/I climb the bridge over the water, . . ." Similarly, the opening lines of "A Poem About George Doty in the Death House" are directed to placing the poet in the scene, introducing his mind, for which George Doty will be an object for meditation: "Lured by the wall, and drawn/To stare . . ./I count the sash and bar. . . ."

Even in the number of poems where the speaker tells his own story, a highly literary language is spoken. Robert Bly frequently inveighs against the iambic line, a term which seems to cover a multitude of sins as he uses it; in *The Green Wall* we observe what he objects to. The angel who comes to open Jesus' tomb and falls in love with earth when he sees a beautiful girl, tells his story thus:

> Now, having heaved the hidden hollow open
> As I was sent to do, seen Jesus waken
> And guided the women there, I wait to rise.

Perhaps no one should expect an angel to speak in the rhythms of the vernacular very well, but the careful alliteration of that first line, the neat shifts of caesuras in the next two remind us of the skilled artist behind this story, the puppet-master pulling these strings. So does the last line of the poem, "As I drift upward dropping a white feather." This is a picture to illustrate a Sunday School homily, and it reflects the same kind of detachment from character and action. What matters is the *point*, the *moral* of the tale, that only human beings can risk human love, not whether the angel is a stereotype.

In *Saint Judas* the struggle of matter with manner continues. Again the most obvious characteristics are organization, control, craft in the use of poetic devices. Again epigraphs accompany the poems as commentaries. Wright announces the book's intention explicitly:

THAT SCARRED TRUTH OF WRETCHEDNESS

To me poetry in this age is the art of stating and examining and evaluating truth. I have tried to shape these poems, singly and as a group, in order to ask some moral questions: Exactly what *is* a good and humane action? And, even if one knows what such an action is, then exactly why should he perform it?

Stating, examining, evaluating, shaping, asking are the work of the discursive reason. Discovery of truth, answers to moral questions, good and humane actions are among the ends of its work, and exactness must be the means. When we come to look at the poetry in *Saint Judas*, however, we see that the struggle of matter with manner is precisely the poet's struggle to break out of the confines of the discursive reason. Crunk says that the most pronounced emotion in *Saint Judas* is guilt. Wright makes the most puzzling figure in all Western literature, but the one we are perhaps quickest to identify ourselves with, the patron saint of his work. On his way to commit suicide, the sin of despair, which Christian tradition has called the *unforgivable* sin, Judas sees another man being beaten by thieves. He forgets himself momentarily, "running to spare his suffering," but then he recalls his own banishment from heaven, the evil he has done, "bread my flesh had eaten,/The kiss that ate my flesh." In full recognition of his situation—still the betrayer, still to commit the sin which confirms his unbridgeable separation from forgiveness—"Flayed without hope,/I held the man for nothing in my arms."

If we reflect on this story as a parable about goodness, we might ask a series of questions: Are good actions those done by good men? Are they actions done only for good reasons? Are good actions those done without consciousness of motive or reward? Are they actions which have a good effect? These are stimulating questions, but they call for answers from the realms of discourse of philosophy or theology. The value or quality of any answer would be assessed according to the tests of consistency, coherence, general applicability, and consequences. We would expect to be able to use the answers as guides for our own actions. But Judas can never be merely a test case for moral philosophy or ethics, and he is not for Wright; he is the supreme riddle, the man who will do evil for pay, but good for nothing, the guilty man who can spring free, however briefly, from the traps of guilt and self-condemnation. Reason does not lead us to make Judas a saint; sainthood itself is a category of existence which rationality cannot comprehend. We understand him, if at all, only through the emotions, only by seeing in ourselves the same capacity for evil or good.

The epigraphs introducing the book warn us that we will be taken into depths where reason alone cannot help. The first is from the Gospel of John 9:34, where the blind man healed by Jesus is being made to account for the miracle to the Pharisees, who wish to condemn Jesus as a sinner. He tries to avoid speaking of Jesus' nature, but, compelled to answer, he becomes more and more affirmative, until he finally says, "If this man were not of God, he could do nothing." The Pharisees then speak the words Wright has made his first epigraph: "They answered and said unto him, thou wast altogether born in sin, and dost thou teach us? And they cast him out."

Can one altogether born in sin teach us? Can his example be something other than a dire warning to the righteous? Wright consistently takes the outcast as his model to test the good, humane action—not by sentimentalizing whores and rapists but by penetrating below the rational into the dark places where good and evil impulses alike begin.

The book's second epigraph brings the self-made outcast, Thoreau, before us. Looking into himself and into the world around him—learning, in Robert Bly's phrase, news of the universe—Thoreau says, "I stop my habitual thinking, as if the plow had suddenly run deeper in its furrow through the crust of the world. How can I go on, who have just stepped over such a bottomless skylight in the bog of my life?" First comes the threat of discontinuity and immobility, but breaking through the crust of the world brings Thoreau good news, and the passage ends, "Heal yourselves, doctors; by God I live."

Again in *Saint Judas* we see all the machinery by which Wright tries to control his poetry and its themes, but we also see that much of it works at cross purposes with them, for what he writes about demands involvement, while the techniques impose a severe detachment. A typical stance, from which he begins "The Revelation" and "The Morality of Poetry," is *musing*: "I stood above the sown and generous sea/Late in the day, to muse about your words." Insights and experiences transmute into *song*, as though to emphasize the protection which aesthetic distance gives.

"The Morality of Poetry" illustrates this conflict of form and content in the book. The poet stands *musing* over a line of Whitman, looking out over the sea. He is above the sea both in physical location and in his intellectual and emotional mood. Poetry concerns him primarily, the sea only secondarily because it is the stuff out of which poetry is made; it is a source of metaphors and images when a mind *reflects* on it. So, in the opening lines of the poem Wright gives us the typical subject-object interaction of poet and scene. The sea takes on a life which reflects the poet's preoccupations; it roars elegies to birds, heaves and groans, casts things up in "slow celebration." Just like a poet making a poem, in short.

The sea, complicated, entangled in itself, becomes an image for the poet's mind working to select and order experience. And as he looks on, "wondering," "counting," examining the images of gulls, sky, and sea, individual images begin to separate out.

> But, high in cloud, a single naked gull
> Shadows a depth in heaven for the eye.
> And, for the ear, under the wail and snarl
> Of groping foghorns and the winds grown old,
> A single human word for love or air
> Gathers the tangled discords up to song.

Through these images the poet penetrates more deeply into his own thought, though not into the scene he stands above. He now makes his first set of generalizations about writing poetry as a moral act: the poet must "Summon the rare word for the rare desire." That word, to be true, must be as clean, spare, streamlined as a gull.

> Before you let a single word escape,
> Starve it in darkness, lash it to the shape
> Of tense wing skimming on the sea alone. . . .

Discipline is the keynote; aescetic control, the lesson the sea teaches. Through "cold lucidity of heart" the poet intended to make "careful rules of song." Now, however, the scene he muses on leads him to further reflection. Wright wants us to understand that rules for making "song" disappear in the presence of nature, but this nature follows all the poetic rules. Thought and scene intermix, but it all becomes like *thought.* When the sun fades, and "thought/By thought the tide heaves, bobbing my words' damp wings," *mind* becomes the moon-wave. The sun charms "my immense irrelevance away," and lures the wings toward the moon, which performs as expected. She is the perfect generator of poetic epithets: "woman or bird," "Flaunting to nothingness

61

the rules I made." She lets "Her cold epistle" fall on the sand, reducing the poet to silence. Here, surely, is the poetic tradition with a vengeance: one more poet worshiping the white goddess!

Caught up in the scene, the poet claims that his voice is gone, his words unfinished: "Where the sea moves the word moves, where the sea/Subsides, the slow word fades with lunar tides." But the maker of images is still in control; we still perceive the mind working on nature, turning it into metaphors. At the end of the poem the poet sends his friend, to whom the poem is dedicated, "echoes of my voice":

> The dithyrambic gestures of the moon,
> Sun-lost, the mind plumed, Dionysian,
> A blue sea-poem, joy, moon-ripple on wave.

All the images of the poem pyramid to celebrate the rich complexity of the moonlit sea, but only as an image of the poet's mind, as echoes of his voice. The result is a lovely poem, a well-made lyric which justifies its abstract title. We know that reality, represented by the sea, is larger than the rules of song; but the poem has also told us that reality comes to us only as a mind works on experience, turning it into a poem. The poet approaches nature reverently, but his point of view has not changed—he still stands above the scene, musing on it.

The lucid moon, the sea's "cold divinities of death and change," the tall stars holding their peace—all keep their distance. Wright wants to approach them, but first he must plumb the depths of being human, which means to be an alien. "In Shame and Humiliation" develops this theme from the starting point of Dostoievsky's Underground Man, who curses the world to convince himself that "he is a man and not a piano-key!" From the insight that man is distinguished from animals in being able to curse—to announce his otherness by denouncing what is over against him, nature, men, God—Wright elaborates the distinctions into a celebration of the effects of consciousness, anger, hatred, murder, the capacity to be wretched. Consciousness, alienation, and language are aspects of the gift of being human, a free agent. Man the outcast, eating the locusts of bitterness, is "nourished by food the righteous cannot eat." The pure and righteous cannot survive, "while the spirit thrives out of its own defeat."

"Man is the listener gone deaf and blind." To see makes one an exile, for though "only the truth is kind," the truth Wright recognizes is what he calls in "The Accusation" "that scarred truth of wretchedness."

These thematic preoccupations require a different kind of form for their working out. Metres and rhythms are generally more relaxed in *Saint Judas* than in *The Green Wall*, but only in the last section of the book, "The Part Nearest Home," where Wright deals explicitly with murderers and traitors, do we feel that being in control is no longer the central concern of the poetry. To write sympathetically of Caryl Chessman, George Doty, and Judas means to appeal from judgment to mercy, from the rational to the nonrational. "In pity for my kind," the refrain with which the poet answers the earth's questions, describes not only his attitude toward other men but also a new understanding of man's place in nature. "The hard stones of the earth are on our side," he says in "The Refusal." The misery man protects himself from, the desolation he has tossed away will hunt him out, "to crack/Out the dried kernel of his heart," and the poet can only plead, "God, God have pity on man apart."

"At the Executed Murderer's Grave" points to the kind of poetry Wright has written in his next two books. Form is there, but it is neither a straitjacket nor a veil for the personal emotions which generate the poem. The central figure is not a persona we call "the poet," but James A. Wright, who introduces himself and his history as a necessary preliminary to addressing himself to the murderer's situation. What he creates is less meditation than exorcism: the past, the contradictory emotions of hatred and pity, disgust, fear come before him and he yields himself to the workings of each. And we trust his letting go before them precisely because Wright himself distrusts the genuineness of his reactions. In the process of making a poem, he expresses his contempt for the result: "I croon my tears at fifty cents per line."

Making poetry has been a method of gaining aesthetic distance from life, for Wright; here ironic detachment from poetry-making itself replaces that other detachment, with the effect of bringing us closer to the raw material. Wright acts at each point to identify and satirize any stance which threatens to become a pose. Thus, while sneering at his "widely printed sighing/Over their pains," he insists that he wastes no pity on the dead nor love on the drunks of Belaire, Ohio—"Christ may restore them whole, for all of me." The dominant emotions of the poem are those of classical tragedy: fear and pity. Wright pities the dying, which is to say himself and everyone alive, for we all stand under sentence of death. More than that, however, we all stand under judgment, for we are none of us justified—"If Belmont County killed him, what of me?"

At stake in "At the Executed Murderer's Grave" is not what constitutes a good or humane action, but which of us can bear to receive justice. Wright now sees nature representing cosmic judgment. Every man stands by the last sea, and "the princes of the sea" come to render judgment; "God's unpitying stars" will hear Wright's confession. Earth is a door he cannot face, a dungeon; the last sea already flows over Ohio, and before these signs of judgment and damnation Wright affirms his communion with Doty, "Dirt of my flesh, defeated, underground."

In the second issue of *The Fifties* (1959), Wright published the first of his new kind of poetry, announcing that he has given up writing "nineteenth century poetry" and repudiating the "classical" poems of his first two books. As Crunk puts it, Wright has finally gotten all the way over that wall, the limitations he imposed on himself by the forms he used and, perhaps even more, by the expectations those forms brought with them. The iambic line, the stanza, the subtle rhyming were vehicles for the quiet, philosophical musing about life which characterized much American and British poetry of the fifties. Though we might have recognized the tug-of-war between forms and what Wright wanted to say, only from the vantage point of his later poetry could we express such dissatisfaction with the earlier; only because he extended his craft can we see that craft was not enough.

The Branch Will Not Break (1963) takes us away from lucidity into darkness. The earlier poems tried to go in the opposite direction. Dark desires and experiences, the darkness of blindness and death dominated the poems, but always to be lifted up into the light and examined there. The epigraph to this book speaks of a land of bliss, where sorrow is taken away and one can be free and happy. This land, seen in dreams, disappears like empty shadow when the morning sun comes. Light, at least the cold light of reason, is the enemy. "Eisenhower's Visit to Franco, 1959" does not simply exploit images of light and dark to satirize two political figures who believe themselves called to fight the forces of darkness, for Eisenhower and Franco *are* the light-bearers, prepared to root out all dark things. But the dark things in the poem include caves, wine in stone jars in villages, things whose darkness promises richness. The light comes from photographers' flash cameras, airport searchlights, a shining circle of police, glittering smiles. "We die of cold, and not of darkness," says the epigraph from Unamuno.

THAT SCARRED TRUTH OF WRETCHEDNESS

Life and energy begin in the dark; the dark restores us if we face it and live with it for its own sake. Yet the images of darkness also keep all their connotations, for Wright: danger, fear, death. Two poems which might be read as companion pieces indicate the complexity of implications associated with darkness. In "Fear Is What Quickens Me," Wright links the "quick eyes" of animals killed by our fathers with wildness and the darkening of the moon. The quickening, coming to life, results from fear and danger. The danger broadens out, conveyed by the images of the darkening moon, the falling of the moon, and the loss of the moon 'to the dark hands of Chicago." In the second stanza the danger and accompanying fear come closer to the poet.

> What is that tall woman doing
> There, in the trees?
> I can hear rabbits and mourning doves whispering together
> In the dark grass, there
> Under the trees.

Nature is alive in the dark grass, that mysterious tall woman seems a threat, the animals whisper secrets the poet cannot know. The final stanza gathers up the emotion of the poem—guilt for the past, fear of death and of some final judgment—by taking us back to those animals with quick eyes who stared about wildly when the moon went dark: "I look about wildly." The poet is quickened, alive, though under a cosmic threat.

In "Beginning" virtually the same key images occur, but they interact in an entirely different fashion. The living moon presides over the scene; it "drops one or two feathers into the field," while "the dark wheat listens." In that listening stillness, even because of it, the moon's young try their wings. Then a slender woman appears between trees, lifts "the lovely shadow/Of her face" and steps into the air. Not only the field, or the moon, or those who inhabit the air, but the air itself is alive. The scene holds the poet immobile, listening, like the wheat. That link continues, for at the end of the poem "The wheat leans back toward its own darkness,/And I lean toward mine." Under the control of the moon, the woman, and the silence, darkness becomes something we can depend on.

The dark things quicken us, but they do not entirely lose their awful threatening quality. If the eyes of ponies "darken with kindness," "small dark eyes" love in secret, "black snow" draws back into itself to restore grass to the earth, and there is a "good darkness/Of women's hands that touch loaves," there is also the darkness of the moon, dark poolrooms, and churches, "dark hands of Chicago," "black waters/of the suburbs," and "American, Plunged into the dark furrows/Of the sea again."

When the poems succeed, they do so typically by linking a few primal images with explicitly stated emotions so that new insights grow out of the resonances set up among them. In "I Was Afraid of Dying" the poet tells of a fear of dying in a dry field, but he has now spent a day walking in damp fields,

> Trying to keep still, listening
> To insects that move patiently.

The fear of death, says Sartre, is the fear that one has never lived. "A field of dry weeds" images a spiritual lack, a confirmation that "I have wasted my life," as Wright says in another poem. He has not thought his way through this fear, however; he has taken it along with him, as part of the burden his unconscious usually bears, on a day's outing. Focusing on the life hidden at his feet, opening to it through stillness and trying to *listen*, he comes across his own fear of dying. What allows him to face his fear also enables him to free himself of it, for he realizes that one lives neither entirely for nor in oneself. A larger life lives *us*, shaping our failures and dead remains to its ends.

> Perhaps they are sampling the fresh dew that gathers slowly
> In empty snail shells
> And in the secret shelters of sparrow feathers fallen on the
>   earth.

Wright gives us emblems of the inner world, where Bly might try to compel our belief in it by the frequency with which he announces it. Wright seems to have fewer opinions about it, to be less preachy about what meanings come from it, but even his political poems have their greatest impact as mediations on the spiritual life. Several of the poems about the inner world carry long, highly circumstantial Wordsworthian titles, like "Lying in a Hammock at William Duffy's Farm in Pine Island, Minnesota," and "As I Step Over a Puddle at the End of Winter, I Think of an Ancient Chinese Governor." Like Wordsworth, Wright wants to anchor these poems in the matter-of-fact, in tiny details of observation. "Lying in a Hammock" reads like pure description until the last line, but then the conclusion—a judgment for which there seems to be no warrant in the foregoing lines—sends us back to look again at the terms in which the scene is rendered. Letting go characterizes the poem; the poet sees a butterfly asleep, hears cowbells following one another, observes horse-droppings blaze up in the sunlight, leans back as a chicken hawk floats above him, looking for home. Creatures are at rest or are going home, floating; things are dormant or acted on. Sunlight turns the horse-droppings into "golden stones," the cows follow the instinct to return to the barn. Crunk says the question the poem never asks directly is:

> How is it possible for there to be so many spiritual emblems, signs, reminders of the path, everywhere, and yet for the man who sees them to have gotten nowhere, to have achieved none of the spiritual tasks that those emblems suggest?[1]

The poem is like Rilke's "Fragment of an Antique Apollo" where celebrating the beauty of the broken sculpture leads the poet to the realization, "You must change your life." In both poems, the insight implies a judgment on the past but not a condemnation; the calm conclusion tells us there is still time to change. The poet has leaned back in the hammock, as he leaned on the darkness in "Beginning." He floats, like the hawk, and now he knows he must look for home.

Despite the darkness of these poems, their penetration into his fears, his despair at being "lost in the beautiful white ruins/Of America," and his suffering, trust seems to be their dominant mood. With the blue jay springing up and down, abandoning himself "To entire delight," the poet knows "the branch will not break." He sees the moon stand up in the darkness, "And I see that it is impossible to die"; and he rejoices with the eagle *This is what I wanted.* Looking at ponies grazing in a field "Suddenly I realize/That if I stepped out of my body I would break/Into blossom."

Happiness comes unbidden. In "Milkweed" he stands in the open, lost in himself, looking out on a farm scene. When he looks down, everything has changed. What was lost is here, imaged in the milkweed filling the air with "delicate creatures/From the other world." Being lost *in himself* turns into having lost *something*, but when he becomes lost in the world around him he discovers that

1. Crunk, "The Work of James Wright," *The Sixties*, no. 8 (Spring 1966): 67–68.

Whatever it was I lost, whatever I wept for
Was a wild, gentle thing, the small dark eyes
Loving me in secret

With *Shall We Gather at the River* (1968), we find ourselves in the presence of something new. In one sense the book simply extends lines of development already seen; the poetic line continues to loosen, the language becomes more colloquial, the inner life of the natural world continues to speak through the poems, certain key themes—darkness, blindness, personal anxieties—run through the book. What is new is a converging of lines, the preoccupation with the outcast, but from a detached point of view, in his first two books, and the opening up to the spiritual world of nature in *The Branch Will Not Break*. In *Shall We Gather at the River*, the poet no longer looks at criminals and imagines himself one, he has become the outcast, opening up to that world as he has to nature. Form as a means of gaining detachment is gone.

Perhaps the clearest way into the book is offered by the title, a line taken from an old revival hymn. In its original context it suggests hope: baptism into a community, the cleansing of sins, being at the throne of God. It also suggests the overcoming of obstacles, passing through the river to get to the other side, to the promised land. All these overtones sound through the book. Introducing Wright as a contributor to *The Fifties* (1959), the editors report, "He says one of the strangest experiences of his life was his first reading as a child of the Blake line: 'The Ohio shall wash my stains from me'." The book conveys a similar strangeness, for the rivers are real—the Mississippi, the Ohio, the Red River, among others—and spiritual symbols at the same time, like Blake's London or Albion.

In "In Response to a Rumor that the Oldest Whorehouse in Wheeling, West Virginia, Has Been Condemned," Wright recalls the whorehouse doors swinging open in early evening and the women pouring down the street "to the river/And into the river." He takes us into a fantasy world of correspondences, Wheeling, West Virginia viewed through a mystic's eyes. The whores become like the river and "pour" into it, but they undergo a change and come out winged, like angels. As though speaking prophecy, he says:

For the river at Wheeling, West Virginia
Has only two shores:
The one in hell, the other
In Bridgeport, Ohio.

THAT SCARRED TRUTH OF WRETCHEDNESS

And nobody would commit suicide, only
To find beyond death
Bridgeport, Ohio.

All of the rivers in the book have one shore in hell, but that at least represents a spiritual state, outright damnation, whereas Bridgeport, Ohio or Minneapolis have not even that much vitality. The poor washed up by winter in Chicago become a black sea, the unfinished Creation, the Sixth Day remaining evening, "a wounded black angel/Forgotten by Genesis." The Ohio River becomes "the dark jubilating/Isaiah of mill and smoke marrow."

The river becomes one term in a series of correspondences: the river and American history, the river and the human bloodstream, the river and the Styx. Wright thus establishes a complex set of references from one to another of these correspondences in such a way as to build up a kind of *paysage moralisé*, a spiritual landscape.

Blood flows in me, but what does it have to do
With the rain that is falling?
In me, scarlet-jacketed armies march into the rain
Across dark fields. My blood lies still,
Indifferent to cannons on the ships of imperialists
Drifting offshore.
Sometimes I have to sleep
In dangerous places, on cliffs underground,
Walls that still hold the whole prints
Of ancient ferns.

The first movement of this poem, "Living by the Red River," links the inner flow of blood with rain falling on the earth as two similar necessities to sustain life. Then history—wars, battles, imperialist warships—becomes internalized as scarlet-jacketed armies march through the body. Finally, the inner danger becomes externalized again, and the poet speaks of sleeping in dangerous places, in hiding. Here he looks back to the ice age and the time when the sea covered midwest America, when the ferns were pressed into rocks. The constant reference back and forth from inner to outer creates a multi-layered image in which the body *becomes* the landscape over which armies have fought and the primal sea and glaciers have passed.

When Wright makes the river an image for American history, he emphasizes the corruption of an originally pure stream. "Three Sentences for a Dead Swan" ends with instructions that the swan's splintered bones should be carried back into the

> Tar and chemical strangled tomb,
> The strange water, the
> Ohio river, that is no tomb to
> Rise from the dead
> From.

In other poems, notably "The Minneapolis Poem," "Gambling in Stateline, Nevada," "To Flood Stage Again," and "The Frontier," we are aware of a correspondence between inner and outer landscapes. The poet is an outcast in a cast-off world, the frontier, the discontinued railroad station in Fargo, North Dakota, the condemned whorehouse in Wheeling.

Standing on the shore, gazing into the dark water are the typical stances the poet takes in the book, not musing from above the water. But he is not a dead man gazing on a mechanistic world. Death reminds us of life, as damnation implies the possibility of salvation. An enigma of the book, apparently as puzzling to Wright as to the reader, is that he can say "My life was never so precious/To me as now," even when he must beg for money to eat. Something valuable in his life, his deepest secret, accompanies him through the wanderings and suffering recorded in the poems. Something exists on behalf of which he can even be an adversary of God: "If I pray,/I lose all meaning." "Men have a right to thank God for their loneliness."

These poems record a struggle with God, to find him but also to maintain one's ways before him. "As a father to his son, as a friend to his friend, be pleased to show mercy, O God," is the epigraph to one poem; in another the poet says he is "longing/For the red spider who is God."

In "Speak," after describing a futile search for Jenny, to whom the book is dedicated and who is addressed in the final poem "To the Muse," the poet lapses into a parody of Ecclesiastes:

> Then I returned rebuffed
> And saw under the sun
> The race not to the swift
> Nor the battle won.

What follows as evidence does not tell of the triumph of the weak and foolish things of this world, but of Sonny Liston taking a dive and

Ernie Doty's being drunk. Jenny has broken her beauty in a whore-house and left her child in a trash can, and the poet can only speak of defeat "in a flat voice.' He has addressed his words to God, and the loosely rhymed lines and biblical-sounding language have given a mock solemnity to the poem which heightens the effect of the flat voice. The final stanza is a prayer directly addressed to God:

> I have gone forward with
> Some, a few lonely some.
> They have fallen to death
> I die with them.
> Lord, I have loved Thy cursed,
> The beauty of Thy house:
> Come down. Come down. Why dost
> Thou hide Thy face?

In the Psalms the speaker frequently recommends himself by affirm-ing that he has loved those whom God loves and hated those the Lord hated. Here the poet identifies those cursed, the outcasts once more, with the beauty of God's house. In "A Prayer in my Sickness," in *Saint Judas*, Wright had invoked God in the same phrase, "Come down. Come down." But there he spoke of being an alien in the self so long that he could not recognize love. In "Speak" he chides God for withholding Himself, asserting that in accompanying the lonely and dying with the dead he has done God's will and justified himself. In "To the Muse" he says:

> Oh Jenny,

> I wish to God I had made this world, this scurvy
> and disastrous place.

The poet, the "I" of these poems, has made himself the supreme outcast, but he has also dared to address God as an adversary who can justify himself before Him. He takes his stand with humanity, this world, whatever the cost: "The anguish of a naked body is more terri-ble/To bear than God." His meaning, the secret life which he maintains against credit managers, cashiers, J. Edgar Hoover, the wish to pray, remains without content, a puzzle to us. The occasional moments of love, the memory of Jenny, that inner world which finds echoes of itself in an open field or a marsh, perhaps even the strange promise that

"The Ohio shall wash my stains from me,"—these confirm the precious-ness of life for Wright.

Wright's *Collected Poems* (1971) draws together most of his pre-viously published poetry, includes a selection of his translations of other poets, and concludes with a section of thirty-one New Poems. The whole book is shaped toward and by these New Poems. It is dedi-cated to "Annie," who appears in a number of them, and the cover and frontispiece have a photograph of a sculpture by Annie Wright called "Two Deer." Deer occur frequently in the poems, joining a number of other dominant images, including the moon, birds, feathers, water, the dead, old men, drunks, and cemeteries. It is Wright's dark world again: nighttime and dream, the world of the outcast, the world of the night fears—loneliness, death, and hell. "Lonely," "alone," "loneliness," and "hell" recur frequently.

Both in form and in subject, the "Two Deer" sculpture belongs with the New Poems; abstract yet rooted in the natural world; rough and concrete in detail, yet suggesting fluidity and lightness; above all, setting up an interplay between the familiar world of nature and memory and the secret inner world of the artist which validates his life. Neither the sculpture nor the poem reveal "meanings" or "ideas" in a discursive sense; at best, they give hints of powers and knowledge which enable the poet to live. Writing of Jonathan Swift's poems, Wright says:

> Here are some songs he lived in, kept
> Secret from almost everyone
> And laid away, while Stella slept,
> Before he slept, and died, alone.

The poem connects Swift's *living in* his poems and their secrecy in a fashion which resists rational comprehension. Somehow the life-affirmation and vitality of writing poetry are increased by keeping them secret from the Yahoos. "Swift is alive in secret. . . ."

The tying together of the *Collected Poems* by the frontispiece and the two introductory poems, "The Quest" and "Sitting in a Small Screenhouse on a Summer Morning," continues in the New Poems themselves. They gather up old subjects, refer back to earlier poems for images, and reach into the new material of the private world. They continue to develop the jagged disconnected speech of the previous volumes, reaching deeper into the secret life even at the risk of being overwhelmed by compulsive images and verbal tics. Poems double back on themselves, words are repeated as though the poet cannot break from their spell. At times the poet intrudes on the poems to announce the difficulties of keeping control.

The key qualities of the New Poems stand clear in the first poem, "The Idea of the Good." The title promises a philosophical discourse working through to the highest level of abstraction. In fact, the poem goes exactly the opposite direction, placing the poet precisely in place and mood, then leading him through memory and reflection to an affirmation of his "precious secret," which the reader is told he cannot know. The poet stands "bone lonely," obsessed by death but begging for "a little life back." Two figures dominate his memory: Judas and Jenny. Both are human beings with their own life stories, but they are also literary creations around whom Wright has organized books. They are both works of his imagination, figures on whom he can project his fears and longings, but they also have separate independent existences. They serve then to remind us that there is a secret at the center of every existence which is not to be broken open but only affirmed.

> I dream of my poor Judas walking along and alone
> And alone and alone and alone till his wound
> Woke and his bowels
> Broke.

The anguish of being alone wakes the wound—the capacity to feel remorse or hurt which defines being human—which in turn leads to a death brought about by too much feeling. The bowels are the seat of the passions in the Bible. Judas is like the poet himself.

> Now once again I take
> My way, my own way,
> Alone till the black
> Rock opens into ground
> And closes and I die.

When he addresses Jenny, he asks for a little life as an exchange for "that unhappy/Book that nobody knows but you/And me." That book, which would seem to be *Shall We Gather at the River*, dedicated to Jenny, is a secret he shares with her, as is this poem. Life, poetry, and secrecy are all one; the poet, like Swift, makes songs to live in. We find ourselves in the presence of something almost magical, a secret ritual by which two people remember a deeper secret. For us there is nothing except the poem, which may set up reverberations in us, give us pleasure and wisdom, without ever revealing the secret. "The Idea of the Good" is something unapproachable, abstract, yet shadowed forth in specific acts and particular lives. The poem, enticing and frustrating as it is, leaves the reader standing outside it with only the one word of advice with which it ends, "Patience."

The reader's access to the poem comes through its music, the play of sounds which link the words together as logic would not. "Bone lonely" sets up one sound sequence which threads through such chime-words as "down" and "now" until it develops the power of obsession in "alone" repeated four times in two lines. The long *O* sound also gives heightened meaning to the essentially visual image of the owl on the grave:

> I want an owl to poise on my grave
> Without sound, but in this mean time
> I want bone feet borne down
> Cold on stone.

A second sound-sequence begins with the repetition of "black rock," recurs in the rhyme of "woke" at the beginning of a line with the one-word line "broke" which follows it, and appears again in "book" and "back."

Only the most obvious and trivial effects of assonance, rhyme, or alliteration can ever be explained. What can be said of sound-patterns in this poem is that they help set up mutually enriching word-patterns which hold before us what is important about Judas and Jenny.

New Poems offers two responses to the secret, *knowing* and *controlling*. "Blue Teal's Mother" weaves the two responses together, making the testing of knowledge both theme and technique. The poet speculates about five blue baby birds, brought home when their parents disappear and lost when a weasel gets them. Those events lead him on to think about the chain of death and destruction they represent: a fox may have killed the parent birds, a weasel got the babies, the weasel is killed for a woman's coat. All that is common knowledge, of no particular importance. "How do I know it was a fox?" "All I know is. . . ."

Behind that knowledge lies another kind, which might be called the knowledge of possibilities, symbolized by the series of transformations which occurs. The birds become the children of the Chevrolet they came home in, the weasel becomes an ermine which becomes a coat "that some women wear dead." Finally, at night and under the spell of drunkenness, the poet feels a tree turn into a slender woman. What the poet knows through these metamorphoses is kinship with nature: "I, too, live,/Even in my pain." That kinship requires that he exert control to abstain from evil, "Give even the living/A chance." The poet makes very limited claims for what he knows, speaking clumsily of the night a bulk tree got in his way and "I knew perfectly well I could have knocked/The bulk tree down." Instead, he embraces it, preferring not to hurt another living thing, and it becomes a woman.

> Stop nagging me. I know
> What I just said.
> It turned into a slender woman.

The poems look two ways. They illustrate a continual opening up to the natural world, to animals, to the lives of the old, the lonely, and the dead, and to paranoid fear and grief within the individual. That is a letting go, often reflected in a deliberate slackening of lines, unpolished diction, clumsy workmanship. In moments of deep emotion, he lets go of his craft, breaking into the well-made poem. In "The Offense" he asks, "And what the hell good does it do me the metre's breaking?" and in "To a Dead Drunk," "(Listen, what rhymes with miracle?)." These are verbal tricks, but this conscious roughening of lines, breaking apart one set of tricks with another set, speaks to his need to loosen control.

The poems also speak of keeping control, a determination to hold in check what is also human—the will to do harm. "Larry" concludes with a warning not to kill an ant, "for she too/Loves her life. Let go, Larry./Let go./Let go." In "So She Said," a woman takes the poet to her bed, out of compassion for his loneliness. He, knowing the meaning of her act, does not use her sexually.

> I did not plow her darknesses,
> Only because I'd rather not
> Flop rampant on the secresies.
> They are easy enough to violate.

"A Secret Gratitude" develops the theme of abstention from evil through an elaborate consideration of the limits of being human. Five deer stand looking at four men. They know and fear them, but it is the men who are caught in the light. Facing the otherness of the deer sharpens the poet's awareness that men are outcasts from nature and spirit alike. The white serenity of nature and the perfect detachment of the angels stand over against the darkness of men. The angels care no more for us than we for ourselves; the moon has abandoned us; "We are a smear of obscenity." We have nothing but power, a capacity to kill and destroy. The poet knows the men can kill the deer and get away with it, having both opportunity and capacity and nothing to check them.

> Man's heart is the rotten yolk of a blacksnake egg
> Corroding, as it is just born, in a pile of dead
> Horse dung.
> I have no use for the human creature.
> He subtly extracts pain awake in his own kind.
> I am born one, out of an accidental hump of chemistry.
> I have no use.

As men "We are capable of anything," but in this case that capability is expressed in respect for life, the withholding of power. The men do not kill the deer.

The poem then turns back to the relation between Eugen Boissevain and Edna St. Vincent Millay, which is the subject of its epigraph. The poet doubts whether the kind, protective Boissevain was human, "From what I know of men." Boissevain becomes a puzzle, a secret, identified with nature in his support for his wife as she gathered

> Leaf, string, anything she could use
> To build her still home of songs
> Within sound of water.

These too are human capabilities: to love and protect, to make a "still home of songs." Boissevain and Millay, representing love and poetry, not in any mythological sense but as capacities of the human creature, effectively answer both man's evil possibilities and the angel's indifference.

Through making a poem the poet grows from the terrible self-hatred of "I have no use for the human creature, . . .I have no use," to trust that humans are capable not only of abstention from evil but of active good. Through the medium of the poem he has also discovered a kinship with Boissevain and Millay. The poem he has made is also a "home of songs" where he can permit his humanity its fullest scope. As if in confirmation of the value of the poem—as secret, as knowledge, as testing ground in which violence and tenderness can both be imagined and acted out—the last stanza describes a waterfall "rippling antiphonally down over/The stones of my poem."

THAT SCARRED TRUTH OF WRETCHEDNESS

Many of the New Poems about human guilt, ignorance, limitation, and depravity reach beyond dissection of human pretension to a tender care for baffled and corrupt man. A larger awareness also runs through the poems, extending the kind of identification of man and the universe which was so evident in *Shall We Gather at the River*. "Small Frogs Killed on a Highway" contrasts these blind creatures hurtling toward their death with the drivers who run over them. The frogs at least are blinded by the light, while

> The drivers burrow backward into dank pools
> Where nothing begets
> Nothing.

And the tadpoles dance, waiting their own time to set out on the quest. Fertility and continuity stand opposed to the sterility of human life. The whole scene of continual destruction is put into a surprising context by the first lines of the poem, which make the frog's action a kind of spiritual search.

> Still,
> I would leap too
> Into the light,
> If I had the chance.

These lines are the pivot on which the poem turns. At first they sound like a concession, as though we overheard the poet in the middle of a thought. Then we notice how "Still" plays off against "leap." The lines may be taken to mean "Even so, I understand why they behave as they do." But they also describe the poet, motionless, in the dark, expressing the wish to leap into the light, taking whatever chance that required. "It is everything, the wet green stalk of the field/On the other side of the road."

The reaching out to incorporate the whole universe into the self becomes most important in "To Harvey, Who Traced the Circulation." The poem builds around an encounter between the poet and a girl.

> One afternoon I lonely found
> Home when a lonely
> Girl slipped her quick
> Shelter down.

In their lovemaking she asks to hear her heart beat in her wrist, he kisses her wrist and speaks of "nothing between us/But the strumming of my pulse yearning/Toward the sea." Laced into this story is an image of the "lonely Brontosaurus," lying down in death, covered with ferns, becoming "secret/Body of the most delicate/Oil, the secret of steel," and making its contribution to the life of the earth and, more directly, to the lives of the two lovers. Their bones have been smoothed into one another by this once-living creature.

In a series of transformations and linking metaphors, familiar from "Living By the Red River," the blood, blue at the wrist, becomes the sea and man becomes a universe. The moon, described in "A Secret Gratitude" as a wounded tigress who tore herself in agony out of the earth's side, rises out of junk; the poet and the woman also rise. The waters are within and without, the pattern of the blood and the pattern of the tides are somehow the same. The love of the two lonely people confirms that pattern.

The water-blood image also operates in "To a Friendly Dun," where the body and the city become identical. The veins gag in the body, and his life may go drifting "face down down the Hudson,/Dead in its own darkness."

> Cold, cold, and the snow blackens the veins
> Of my city, my love, my dark city, the ocean of
> Darkness, where we are all
> Lonely together.

Perhaps the most complex poem in the New Poems is "Many of our Waters: Variations on a Poem by a Black Child." It draws together most of the themes which run through the collection and, in its free, loose impressionistic form, images the interaction of theme and form. The poem has seven sections of varying lengths and takes its start from a journal entry which the poet makes into a found poem. The Black child Garnie Braxton, who has presided over New Poems as Jenny did those of *Shall We Gather By the River*, has looked at a group of workers digging the foundations of a skyscraper. He fantasizes about a blind boy riding a bicycle into the water of the foundation-hole, which turns into acid.

> he drown
> he die
> and then
> they bury him
> up.

The first variation takes the poet back to the Ohio River, which is where he was born, where he wants to spend eternity in hell, and home. It is rotten now, though "Ohio" means "beautiful river." Returning to the river reminds him of two lines by another American poet, "writing about a lonely girl's lovely place."

> He cried out, "That reeking slit, wide, soft, and lecherous,
> From which we bleed, and into which we drown."

All the key correspondences have been made: home, hell, beauty which has turned rotten, the human body, and the river. He apostrophizes the river as "my secret and lovely place, . . . my bareass beach," but breaks into these developing lines to say that this is not a poem or apology to the muse but "the cold-blooded plea of a homesick vampire/To his brother and friend." Before we can puzzle out what is happening, the poet goes on to ask that, if the preceding lines do not matter to us, we not go on listening. "Please leave the poem./Thank you."

The poem itself picks up again when he continues his apostrophe to the Ohio, now back-broken, once beautiful and young. "Now all I am is a poet,/Just like you." He recalls the work of the river as healing and cleaning, but now he is lonesome, sick, frightened, "And I don't know/ Why./*help*.

In the third section, poetry becomes the stream, "the clear pure word." The poet wants to write "The poetry of a grown man," which means working slowly, cursing oneself into black silence, enduring suffering silently. What happens to the grown man is like what Garnie had imagined for the poor boy who drowns: "He shuts up./He dies./He grows." In the fourth section, the only poetry he wants is to lie down with his love, who comes in the rain and is "a little ripple of rain/On a small waterfall."

The fifth and sixth sections explore the poet's relationships with Garnie, Garnie's brother Kinny, Gemela, and his love. What matters is the exchange between the poet and Garnie, "Can Kinny come too?/I aint got nothing but my brother./. . . Neither have I, get the hell over here."

The streams—rivers, the pure stream of poetry, the rainfall associated with love—lead to the mountain pool, a gathering of waters. The pool is where the deer have come to drink, not being frightened off by the poet and his love, who bathe there naked. "For once in our lives we did not frighten/The creation." They are signs of a benediction, living their own lives without fear and giving confidence and solace to outcast man. The poet has turned to the deer in several of the poems as a sign of the balanced natural life, independent of man, man's victim, but also a bearer of something like grace to man. Here their appearance at the pool is a sign that things are gathering together. From the description of that scene the poet turns to address his brother, to whom the poem is dedicated. The poet knows what he wants, to live his life, but he cannot "unless you live yours."

The brother and the waters are associated in the poet's mind, because they are all he has—a human connection and a touch with nature. The poem has been a disconnected, uncontrolled attempt to uncover knowledge of what the poet wants, and its method itself helps show him what that is. He has been "slicking into my own words/The beautiful language of my friends," making a work which is the result of the interpenetrations of man and nature, the waters of the Ohio and the stream of poetry, the mixing of many people's words. When the waters break, they break in a woman's body and a man's heart—they are that inner stream, the blood, the amniotic fluid which washes us into life, and the waters of our native country, once pure but now rotted. The poet's final association links the waters with pity:

> Pity so old and alone, it is not alone, yours or mine,
> The pity of rivers and children, the pity of brothers, the pity
> Of our country, which is our lives.

The poet calls "Many of Our Waters" a "scattering poem," and the phrase is apt. Associations are arbitrary, false connections to any but a mind under fierce pressure. The language is elegant and graceless by turns; images and sections seem to fall together at random rather than to take their place in a planned work. The New Poems are not written in the careful, precise language of indictment but in the broken stuttering of confession—"I don't know," "I have no use," "and what the hell good does it do me the metre's breaking?" When the poems are most effective, the stuttering breaks into affirmation, an intense identification with the whole creation. The final poem in the *Collected Poems* exemplifies this. Starting with clipped, angry fragments, announcing that everybody will die "in a loneliness/I can't imagine and a pain/I don't know," the poet describes catching, killing, and eating a Northern Pike. Though he does not wish to kill, he has to go on living, so he accepts his task. But because his business is with life, which only sustains itself on the death of others, he makes a ritual of the eating of the fish, praying for the muskrats, the ripples made by crawdads under water:

> We prayed for the game warden's blindness.
> We prayed for the road home.
> We ate the fish.
> There must be something very beautiful in my body,
> I am so happy.

Crunk said that while the most pronounced emotion in *Saint Judas* is guilt, the book also reveals "a remarkable and rare good-will" toward the self, Wright's conviction that his self is significant and worthwhile. The reviewer for the *Times Literary Supplement* said of *Shall We Gather at the River*, "the omnipresence of despair in these poems takes us painfully beyond the normal definitions of literature." Those comments trace a remarkable line of development. Wright has let go utterly; all the tight form of his earliest work has disappeared, and we see a man defenseless before experience, his human frailty, and his care for others. At times the guilt seems to have extinguished all goodwill toward the self, but it returns in goodwill toward others, or in gratitude for a sign of beatitude.

It is rare that a man can use loneliness, fear, and grief as means to love of the universe and other people. To use Wright's favorite imagery again, it is as though he had blocked and dammed all the usual outlets of feeling, all the surface runoff which might go into making interesting poetry, concentrating the flow instead through very few, but deepcut, channels. American guilt, personal guilt, fear approaching paranoia, all build up to unbearable intensity before discharging their energy in a phrase—"I ain't got nothing but my brother"—or an image of two deer drinking at a pool in the company of a man and woman who do not frighten the creation.

5

The Inner War

Two stages are readily discernible in William Everson's life as a poet. For fifteen years he published poetry as William Everson—farmer, printer, conscientious objector of no particular religious persuasion in World War II; for nearly twenty years he was Brother Antoninus—convert to Catholicism, Dominican lay brother. That second state represented by the name in religion is now over, since he has given up his annual vows as an oblate, left the Order, and married.

The pre-Catholic poetry reflects the same preoccupations which mark all his later work. It is rooted in awful awareness of nature and history, the two matrices in which man either finds himself or knows himself trapped. Both nature and history are violent; both represent outwardly and universally the inner war which Everson experiences. Kenneth Rexroth says in his introduction to *The Residual Years* that all of Everson's poetry, including the later, Catholic poetry, "is concerned with the drama of his own self, rising and falling along the sine curve of life. . . ." Coming to terms with the self also means coming to terms with the savagery of men and the savagery of the natural world. And poetry is both a means of coming to terms and the product of the conflicts out of which the self is being shaped. Poetry has pattern, created by the tug and pull of emotions and events, refined and perfected in the frustration of human fallibility and incapacity. "The Answer," a poem from *The Impossible Choices* (1940—1946), explores these themes. The poet labors over his lines, drawing on the pain which has afflicted him from birth—failure, guilt, the tyranny of sex—but no poem comes, "nothing converges." Only later, when some sense experience or casual word evokes a response from the inner depths, do "the inner locks open." Conscious labor is replaced by unconscious growth: "The thought stirs in its seed;/The images flower"; and the poem emerges,

> Freighted with judgment,
> Swung out of the possible into the actual,
> As one man's insight matches mankind's at the midpoint of
>   language;
> And the meeting minds reduplicate in the running vowel
> Their common concern.

The inner war is a necessary prelude to the act of creation, but creation itself comes from those depths in the self where individual and race meet, where convergence occurs. The poem does not belong to the poet alone; it confirms and is confirmed by the language of the race.

> Then here rides his triumph:
> Caught in his doom he had only his anguish,
> But the human pattern imposes across his stammering mind
> Its correctional hand.

"Delicate structure," "midpoint of language," "the human pattern": all speak of the individual's link with others, but for Everson these links are most frequently created by guilt and violence, the outer wars which reflect the inner. In "Attila" and "Fish-Eaters" Everson speaks of the violent past from which individuals and social forms alike spring. Attila's outer wars failed—though only because there have been so many others—but he has made his mark on the deeps of life, in the genes of the race and in the unconscious. The poet cannot trace his blood to its single source; it has mingled in thousands as a result of conquest, war, and lust. But, thinking of the fish-eaters, he knows that what he wants, his longing for peace, somehow has its roots in that past he must explore and affirm: "I, the living heir of the bloodiest men of all Europe."

What has made structure—the human pattern, language, social institutions—is violence. In "The Roots" the poet meditates on the English, gaunt raiders, broken in turn by waves of conquest, who shape the words of our language from their history: ". . . The single rhythm of the ancient blood/Remembers the anguish, the hate and desire." Trying to write, the poet feels behind him this trial and error, the shaping of sounds for experience, the awareness of generations coming to form in his mind.

A poem has both structure and freedom; it is both personal and universal; it is made from the stuff of violence but transformed into peace and beauty; it is a midpoint of language where minds meet. A poem grows out of the tangle and struggle of opposites. Light comes out of darkness: "I feel the power rising out of the dark sources,/Those unknown springs in the sea-floor of the self." *War* is a constant motif in the poetry, whether Everson is writing about the act of making poetry, his consciousness of history, or his response to the natural world. The poem "Sun" begins "Season on Season the sun raiding the valley/Drowns it in light." The storms speak "furious words" and "syllables of thunder"; the music of nature, like the music of poetry, grows out of the dark impulses, danger, destruction.

Everything is at war, but the poet's end is to find peace without sloth. The early acts of Everson's drama of the self are played out against the backdrop of the rise of fascism in Europe and the approaching world war. Two poems in particular memorialize the drama: "The Sides of a Mind" and "Invocation." In the first, the spiritual struggle expressed in the conflict of *sides* of a mind parallels the physical struggles being played out in war, the march of squadrons, and "the smell of misery and rot and the filth of the poor." Behind the battle to build shining cities and obliterate poverty there still lies the doubt that any human action matters. "But there is no God, nor was ever a God,/And that is the root of our trouble." Working over his futile poem, the poet feels the power to write surging in him but lacks a theme: "Belief made foolish, the pitiless hunger unfulfilled,/The mind crying for anchor." He surveys his heritage and knows only guilt and inadequacy; he turns to nature and sees only the destruction on which his life is predicated. Working in the fields, breathing, eating, his body is inescapably engaged in warfare against other creatures.

> Every sucking breath that I drew
> The long border of warfare ran down my lungs,
> Furious soldiers of my blood warring and killing, . . .

The poet turns inward so radically that he becomes conscious of the oozing of his pores, the sloughing of dead skin from his feet, and the growing of his nails, and asks whether this ugly decay can justify his poetry. The poem reaches two conclusions, the first that "life feeds on life," so that what we make of our existence means everything and nothing. This thematic rounding off leaves unresolved the conflict represented by the "sides of the mind." The second conclusion loses the conflict in a lyrical celebration of the close of a decade and the opening of something new. Nature for itself, not as a symbol of any inner meaning, soothes the poet; the night flows and the river rolls, "the decade wears itself out," and the unsubstantiated hope for the future closes the poem.

"Invocation" also sums up a decade, in this case the completion of the poet's third decade. Now, however, he has made his affirmations, recorded for example in "The Vow," never to take life wantonly, to atone in his soul for the past he had no control over, to show pity and mercy to all life precisely because he knows its ultimate dissolution. He now sees the spring fructification, the summer fulfillment of nature, and asks for himself a part in that fertility and harvest. He is still at war, "in which neither the foe nor myself is known," a war within the self which finds its double in the war between men. To answer his question "And I? What am I?" the poet must strip away the ease and pleasure, the lack of imagination, the habitual frameworks which conceal the warfare.

There runs the war,
In the half-perceived but unattended,
There at the marginal edge of perception,
There must it be met.

He promises his pity for all living things, so that the spirit will be cleansed, the ego chastened, the senses hushed. He pictures the terrible struggle of evolution, where the self is locked in its inner struggle and "the extensional conflict," but where the perception of its need and its partial attainment can partially redeem the waste of the past. And out of that vision of the war of evolution he prays that his thirtieth year might yield him fulfillment.

Of Everson's early poetry it might be said that his theme is finding a form, while his forms express a persistent struggle to find a theme. The war in the self has as its purpose finding a truth to speak and to live by. But war is always destructive; Everson's poetry is marked by disgust for the physical—especially human sexuality—shame, guilt, imperfectly controlled violence. That this should be so in the writing of one so sensitive to the times in which he lives is not to be wondered at. What he longs for is meaningful pattern, a framework within which life makes sense. History provides one framework, nature another, and many of Everson's poems grow out of the attempt to measure and value the self against the patterns of family history, racial history, or natural history.

The verse patterns and language he uses in these poems illustrate the theme-form problem. He favors long poem-sequences where the separate stanzas and parts often relate to each other like separate poems within a book. End-rhyme or regular metrical patterns rarely occur; instead Everson uses alternations of long and short lines to represent the rise and fall of emotion or activity. Lines are frequently built up in the loose parallelism of the Hebrew Psalms. Phrases and words modify each other simply by being placed side by side. The poetry frequently tends toward slackness—in the line, the stanza, and poem—which duplicates the emotional sprawl. The language he uses serves to counteract this effect, but not without exacting its own price. Anglo-Saxon monosyllables predominate, often harsh, blunt words which convey images and feelings through tactile impressions. Nearly every noun has its adjective, but often they are past participles which lend a sense of physical action to the phrase.

> The whispering wind,
> The erect and tensile filaments of weeds,
> The fallen leaf,
> Half-consumed near the igneous rock,
> All keep accordance,
> Strung on the rays that leave no trace,
> But sift out the hours
> Purling across the deaf stones,
> While the exactitude of each entering star
> Chronicles the dark.
>
> ("A Privacy of Speech" IX)

Intense but unfocused emotion, language in which physical reality and intellectual abstractions jostle with one another, form and theme in search of one another, an aura of violence surrounding even the most pastoral poems: these are the characteristics of Everson's earliest verse. Perhaps no recent poet better exemplifies the longing for and resistance to form.

In 1949 William Everson became a Roman Catholic, in 1950 he began working with the poor as part of the Catholic Worker movement, and in 1951 he entered a Dominican monastery. An intense conversion led to a series of callings, first away from secular success, and finally away from the secular life itself. With his new name, symbolizing a new life and changed nature, Brother Antoninus also received a new, tight, and finely articulated framework into which he needed to fit his whole life. His next book of poems, *The Crooked Lines of God: Poems 1949–1954*, testifies to the importance of that framework, as do the "Pages from an Unpublished Autobiography" which appeared in *Ramparts* in September, 1962, and the interviews he has given.

> The first thing about a vocation is that there is a need for perfection. . . . If you come to the religious life, you come to do sacrifice. This is imperative. If this is not understood, woe to the man who comes; if his inner search, his grasp of reality, does not exceed his other concerns, even his art becomes a trifling thing. [1]

The terms in which Brother Antoninus describes the religious life set the conditions for a more intense inner war than he has experienced before, except that the adversaries cannot claim an equal right to win. To practice the vocation of artist in opposition to the religious vocation is to commit the sin of disobedience. The dedication of the artist becomes willful pride. God writes straight; man—the poet—writes crooked. "My crooked lines, tortured between grace and the depraved human heart (my heart) gouge out the screed of my defection. Everywhere about me the straight writing hems me in, compresses me, flattens my will." [2]

The Crooked Lines of God shows a number of organizing principles at work. There is, of course, Roman Catholic theology, stressed and heightened by the convert's zeal. Following that organizing principle, Brother Antoninus has arranged the poems in three parts, "each corresponding to a particular phase of spiritual development, and each dominated, more or less, by the psychology of a particular saint." The first section he sees dominated by the psychology of Saint Augustine, focusing on guilt, repentance, and the contemplation of the Passion; the second section, corresponding to his time with the Catholic Worker, he sees as Franciscan in psychology; the third is Dominican, moving through "the full development of the erotic religious psychology of the Spanish Baroque." This three-part division also roots in Brother Antoninus's development chronologically, taking us from the conversion through its first fruits, to the monastery and to the point where the

1. Brother Antoninus, "The Artist and the Religious Life," *The American Benedictine Review* 11, 3–4 (Sept.–Dec. 1960): 233–34.
2. Brother Antoninus, "Foreword" to *The Crooked Lines of God* (Detroit: University of Detroit Press, 1959).

clash of crooked and straight choke out poetry. Finally, Brother Antoninus set the type for the book, giving, as we shall consider later, yet another important shaping influence on the poetry, "concretizing" the spiritual states it testifies to.

The book opens with "Triptych for the Living," the first poems of his conversion, and they reflect the intense compression of that subjective experience in the form of the Christmas story, the mature, skeptical mind reflecting on and appropriating the most naive elements of the Christian mythos.

"The Uncouth" is a meditation on the shepherds to whom the angel announced the birth of Christ. The subject is almost mandatory for the Christian poet, but for that reason a successful handling is difficult. The story always raises the same questions, approached and answered in hundreds of poems and thousands of sermons each Christmastide: Why were these simple people first given the Good News? What does this story say to our own time? Unfortunately, the range of responses to these questions has narrowed down over the years. W. H. Auden makes the shepherds represent the *Lumpenproletariat*, a void to be filled, a force to be given direction. That is one kind of updating. Brother Antoninus gives us another kind—straightforward, unironic—making the shepherds a symbol for the perennial outcast, the uncouth who is unknown and unknowing. Once this connection is made, however, there is nothing more to do with it—no shock of recognition, no admiration of a witty comparison, nothing but the working out of details.

Recognizing this, Antoninus paints a picture reminiscent of an altar-panel, where our interest is engaged more by craftsmanship than by the story. The scene becomes California, the shepherds become the sheepherders, "in the folklore of the West . . . of all types the most low."

> As for them, the herdsmen,
> They'd rather hug out the year on a juniper ridge
> Than enter now, where the hard-bitten settlers
> Fenced their acres; where the merchants
> Wheedled the meager gain of summer;
> Where the brindled mastiffs
> Mauled the wethers.

They become types of the "prime, animal amplitude for life," the representation of unchanneled energy, the body and "naked intelligence" awaiting a soul. Grace comes first to them, in Antoninus's poem, *because* they have retained the purity of ignorance and have no knowledge of either the world or the angel.

Since Antoninus leaves the story untouched, except to place it in an American setting, we must look to the details of form to determine whether he has made something new. The poem has six stanzas of varying lengths, from one line to thirteen, loose verse paragraphs built on irregular iambic lines. Only the diction gives any sense of energy to the poem, and it is rooted in physical description, monosyllables, and strong verbs. Some coined words effectively surprise the reader: "pastures/Greened again with good verdure," "Wind northed for cold," "wilderness-hearted earth." Alliteration and assonance operate to give the poem a quiet music.

When we compare this poem, a quiet, pious rendering of a traditional Christian story, with the prose account of its genesis, we see some of the difficulties Antoninus faces in working with the framework he has chosen. In "Pages from an Unpublished Autobiography" he speaks of attending midnight mass, Christmas of 1948, sitting in the church and feeling his customary estrangement from it. He smells "the resinous scent of fir trees" coming from the crib which the nuns had set up in the cathedral. He seizes on the scent with "true realization," and without the rebellion it would ordinarily call up. "Now out of the greatness of my need I sensed in it something of a verification, a kind of indeterminate warrant that I need not fear, were I to come to Christ, that He would exact the dreaded renunciation of my natural world." [3] The verification, only a scent mixed with the incense, draws him into meditation on the scene in the crib. He reflects on the shepherds until "I saw the correlation." This, the key to his conversion, is also the key to the poem; the California sheepherder becomes a confirmation of the meaning of the Incarnation, for the Good News comes first to the man of the wilderness, the ignorant sheepherder subdued to what he works in. All this Antoninus renders for us through constant reference to the odors of the fir and the recalled odors of the sheepherders. The *evidence* which wins his assent to Christianity comes though "the odor of fir, the memory of sheepdung and mutton grease, cutting across the closed interior air of the Cathedral." After the logical structure of a faith has been affirmed, he says, there remains a blankness of those

3. Brother Antoninus, "Pages from an Unpublished Autobiography," *Ramparts* (September 1962):60.

areas of association "which make in the mind the living thing a religion must be," and this blank filled for him when the odor of fir persuaded him that Christ would not deprive him of "the natural kingdom and the great sustaining Cosmos. . . ." [4]

Turning from the crib to the woman beside him, whom he loves, the poet reflects on the feminine receptivity to the Mystery. The woman becomes a symbol for intuition, openness, "vibrant expectancy." Alternating between her innocent waiting and the crude primitive subjectivity of the sheepherder, Antoninus weaves his meditation, searching for the correlations. In turn he stands in the Mystery of Christ and the Mystery of the Church: "The once sinister Church, seen only as evil, becomes in a trice the resplendent Mother of Men, the Christ as pure beneficence, and he skips in singing." [5]

Paraphrasing his description of the moment of conversion cannot do Antoninus justice. In a few pages he shows us the convergence of forces and experiences and the discovery of "correlations" so vividly that we stand within the conversion situation with him. Intellectual insights and affirmations of faith receive some final confirmation for him through his senses; the smell of fir and the remembered smell of sheepherders become signatures for a spiritual truth. And we participate in this with him. Unfortunately, the poem which grows out of this experience is thin and abstract by comparison. Perhaps the simplest explanation for the difference is that the autobiographical passages must be in the first person, the discoveries must be personal, while the third-person telling in the poem distances events. But, more importantly, there is a world of difference between discovering a correlation or link in one's past which brings a truth home to oneself, and elevating that correlation into a general truth. Antoninus tries to translate the emotional and spiritual profundity of his experience into a rational profundity in the poem, and it does not work.

In this we see the chief difficulty facing Brother Antoninus as a poet and us as his readers. The conversion has been accomplished and is in the past:

> Nothing remains to show now but the poetry, and what is that? Something of the energy is contained there, but also something of the shapelessness, something persisting in the mystery of form,

4. Ibid., p. 61.
5. Ibid., p. 64.

the mystery which blankets and obscures the outline of its temporality, but somehow releases the abiding energy, the force, and the inherent motive that made the act what it was. [6]

Form is ambiguous for Antoninus. Energy and shapelessness come together; the mystery of form stands over against them, acting to release energy but also to obscure and blanket the "outline of its temporality," which apparently means all the slight details of sensory experience, the stuff out of which poetry, and conversions, is made. Form comes *ab extra*, imposed by a theory or a theology. The poems must be introduced with a Foreword to blanket and obscure the torment of unworthy thoughts and human temptations by announcing that the crooked lines will eventually be made straight. The Foreword reports that the inner war, out of which the poems come, is over, or has ended in armistice.

"The Coming" and "The Wise," the other poems of the Triptych, are like "The Uncouth" in employing vigorous, kinesthetic language to explore relatively simple correlations between past and present. The "freshness, raciness and energy of immediate observation," which Samuel Johnson demanded of poetry, are there in abundance, but we must conclude, also with Johnson, that so far as theme is concerned "there is no nature, for there is nothing new." What is said is familiar, orthodox.

A number of problems arise in any treatment of biblical stories. The most obvious is that one has little latitude with a sacred fable; the details must be faithfully reproduced or any deviation thoroughly justified by its clever contemporaneity. Of course, in the richest literature, details occur for themselves and for the deeper significance they offer the rest of the work, but when the details of a story are so sacred that the only acceptable use of the artist's imagination is to make every one of them plausible in a new telling, no matter what the demands of the new work are, we see the heaviest weight of tradition.

Perhaps a more difficult problem to deal with for the artist who wishes to explore Christian themes is one we find in the New Testament itself, namely, that every action and speech must be explained through the benefit of hindsight, by reference to types and prophesies. So every surprising act or word of Jesus is explained by reference to the crucifixion and resurrection which are in the future, from the narrative's point

6. Ibid., p. 58.

of view, but already accomplished for the narrator. Or the hard sayings are explained as fulfilling a prophesy from the Old Testament. Saint Paul's reading of the Old Testament as providing types and shadows of Christ illustrates the difficulty of reading a text free of this sacralizing tendency.

A third problem in dealing with a sacred fable is that it must be made to bear theological or spiritual freight. It must mean more than the events themselves. Frequently the artist meets this demand by a resort to dramatic irony of the "had-we-but-known!" kind, underplaying the events while hinting at their cosmic significance. T. S. Eliot's "The Magi" is an example of the type, as are "Triptych for the Living" and other poems in *The Crooked Lines of God*. The generalizing of "The Flight in the Desert" illustrates the point:

> This was the first of his goings forth into the wilderness
>   of the world.
> There was much to follow: much of portent, much of dread.
> But what was so meek then and so mere, so slight and strength-
>   less,
> (Too tender, almost, to be touched)—what they nervously guarded
> Guarded them. As we, each day, from the lifted chalice,
> That fragile Bread the mildest tongue subsumes,
> To be taken out in the blatant kingdom,
> Where Herod sweats, and his deft henchmen
> Riffle the tabloids—that keeps us.

The look forward here requires turning the infant Jesus and Herod into symbols at the cost of their humanity. So much is made of the deeper significance of the flight into the desert that we lose sight of the personal drama, and even the final stanza, picturing the Holy Family around a campfire while Jesus feeds at his mother's breast, fails to persuade us that these are real people. Anyone reflecting on his sacred stories will discern in them both a universal and individual significance; seeing the world's history and the history of his own life converging in each story. It is harder to recognize that what gives them their vigor is that they are first of all the history of the people they speak about. In "Gethsemani" Brother Antoninus describes Christ fainting with fear as He contemplates the approaching crucifixion. The language is vivid and excites our compassion, but then the theological tidying-up begins. "Power had proved his Godhead," the poet says,

But that the God was man,
That the man could faint,
This the world must know.

The human suffering becomes an object lesson and loses its credibility in the process. "Whatever the world will suffer/Is here foresuffered now." The second and third parts of this long poem become steadily more discursive and correspondingly less interesting poetically. Rhetorical questions and exclamations become the chief devices for importing excitement into the poem. Finally the object lesson swallows everything else.

His subject has deep importance to Brother Antoninus, and he clearly has brought to it a wealth of reading and reflection. He is personally engaged throughout the work, but the poem is not personal and fails to engage the reader personally, for where there should be discovery and revelation, there is only explication.

When Coleridge published his "Reflections on Having Left a Place of Retirement," he attached to it the epigraph *sermoni propriora*, "in his own voice," which Charles Lamb preferred to translate as "properer for a sermon." For though Coleridge was deeply engaged with his reflections—tentative religious opinions and ideas and resolutions for future action—poetic form was more a convenience than a necessity for them. For the poet to speak "in his own voice" will not make the result poetry, if the voice he uses is a schoolteacher's or the village explainer's. A constant difficulty with Brother Antoninus's poetry is precisely that what matters most to him, what brought him to his faith and his vocation as a Dominican Friar, cannot be directly translated into poetry. When he speaks *semoni propriora* as a Dominican, what he says may be "properer for a sermon." At least, in the practice of his art, a tension actually exists between the demands of form and those of content.

The short, choppy line and a largely Anglo-Saxon vocabulary characterized Brother Antoninus's pre-Catholic poetry, as it does much of his later work. In *The Crooked Lines of God* he also tries a number of *canticles*, songlike poems composed in long, flowing lines. Here the influence of Catholic liturgy is most clearly seen, but it is enriched by other streams which have fed the poet, including Robinson Jeffers, Whitman, and the Song of Songs which has such a direct influence on the liturgy. The long accentual line and loose parallelism of the canticle form offer an ideal medium for one of Antoninus's favorite themes, celebrating the plenitude of nature. His "Canticle to the Waterbirds" in the second section of the book, glories in the creation, symbolized by the strange waterbirds of California. The early stanzas of the poem illustrate what Gerard Manley Hopkins meant when he spoke of "stress" and "idiom," whatever strongly accentuated individuality and set one thing off from another, and "inscape," how the details of external nature reflect an inner, spiritual shape.

> Clack your beaks you cormorants and kittiwakes,
> North on those rock-croppings finger-jutted into the rough Pacific surge;
> You migratory terns and pipers who leave but the temporal claw-track written on sandbars there of your presence;
>
> .   .   .
>
> Break wide your harsh and salt-encrusted beaks unmade for song
> And say a praise up to the Lord.

Detail, difference, individuality, and their beauty take the center of the poem, but once again Antoninus turns from describing things as he sees and loves them to explaining what they are *there* for. And a long, loose line is the worst possible medium for discursive writing: "But mostly it is your way you bear existence wholly within the context of His utter will and are untroubled."

In the final section of his book, Brother Antoninus explores most freely the sensual language and compressed intensity which were common to his earliest poetry. Here he takes his warrant from the Spanish Baroque and particularly from Saint John of the Cross and Saint Teresa of Avila. Saint John can be a particularly lucky influence on a poet still newly converted enough to suffer from scruples about literary creation, for he was able to separate the system-building aspects of his theology from the intense personal experience from which it drew its evidence. *The Ascent to Mount·Carmel* and *The Dark Night of the Soul* are prose treatises on the spiritual life; the poems render the sensual and emotional experience of religious ecstasy. And, as Saint John says in the preface to *The Ascent to Mount Carmel*, all the stages of the spiritual journey to be explicated in the prose work are revealed in one poem in which the soul perceives itself as the Bride of Christ.

His influences allow Brother Antoninus to write about violence and sex, subjects which have always held a threatening fascination for him. Now he can bring them together, as in his canticle for Mary Magdalene, and speak of "A Savagery of Love." Mary Magdalene's saintly purity, her sacrificial love of Christ, are the redirecting of her sexuality, not its abnegation. The crucifixion becomes truly the Passion of Christ as we view it through her eyes, taking on some of the sexual significance of suffering for love of others. As Mary Magdalene poured out her body for the delight of others, she poured out the oil to anoint Christ's feet and finally pours out her grief at the foot of the cross. As her sexual nature is completed when her body has been penetrated, so Antoninus makes the lance's penetration of Christ's body a symbol for the completion of His Passion, love of mankind.

> What plenitude of power in passion loosed,
> When the Christ-love and the Christ-death
> Find the Love-death of the Cross!

If sex and violence threaten Brother Antoninus, following the example of Saint John of the Cross gives him a way to exploit the themes and still keep distance between this poetry and his earlier, pre-Catholic work, for in these poems he imagines himself feminine, receiving the mark of God as the barren doe receives the blaze of the buck. In "A Canticle to the Christ in the Holy Eucharist" he speaks of Christ as the mark, the kill, the wound, and describes himself sucking the wound as a fawn sucks milk from its mother. "Thy word in my heart was the start of the buck that is sourced in the doe." Sexual conquest unites violence and sensuality; when God is the conqueror, the man who must otherwise assert his aggressiveness through sexual conquest may justify his passivity and even pray "Annul in me my manhood, Lord, and make/Me woman-sexed and weak." At the risk of appearing to psychoanalyze or explain away Brother Antoninus's poetry, we may say that these poems of the final section of the book attempt to sublimate material and personal drives which have been the source of both anxiety and intense power in his earlier work. These personal issues are by no means resolved through the poetry, though the intensity of the struggle confirms his wish to change his nature. They are among the most striking of his poems, but they testify eloquently to the constrictions which finally shut off the poetic flow with which his conversion began.

Brother Antoninus wanted to create a double work of poetry which would balance out his earlier work. In this plan either his inspiration or God failed him. What stands out clearly is how the claims of the religious life and those of the artistic impulse interact to provide what he calls "creative tension," the "tension which is union."

Whether speaking about the religious life, artistic creation, or the structure of the human psyche, Brother Antoninus always begins with paired opposites: active and contemplative, conscious and unconscious, rational and nonrational, intellect and imagination, male and female. In discussing the tensions which beset the artist in a religious community, he develops an extended and evocative contrast between the institutional and the charismatic. This becomes the key distinction for talking about all the creative tensions he experiences; the tug between these two characterizes the church as well as the individual within it. "Any religion can only develop by refining the tension between its charismatic and institutional elements. . . .When the charismatic finally breaks through an institutional matrix and makes its pronouncement, it brings down upon itself the whole wrath of an almost unconscious terror from the opposite side."[7]

It would be unfair to treat this distinction as an attempt to speak with philosophical precision, for Brother Antoninus is using it to discover how the conflicts and interactions of opposites have fructified his own life and where they have caused paralysis. "Charismatic" as he uses it always roots back to the literal meaning of the word, a divinely inspired gift of supernatural power or a capacity to lead others. The charismatic side he identifies, therefore, with the Dionysian, the irrational, the artistic, the creative, and the mystical. Inwardness, contemplation, and the imagination are all associated with it. "The artist is an imaginative man, and the whole mode of an artist is freedom. The imagination, strictly speaking, knows no laws." [8] The charismatic must always be ambiguous and dangerous; it always threatens to dissipate its gifts in the pursuit of freedom.

For Brother Antoninus the struggle between religion and art seems far less the result of a tension between the charismatic and the institutional, though that plays its part, than between contrary aspects of the charismatic itself. The charisma presses toward fulfillment of its own nature, toward some kind of perfection. Here is the source of a deep conflict within the charismatic as Brother Antoninus understands it, for if the artist fulfills his gift through freedom, the religious man fulfills

7. Brother Antoninus, "The Artist and the Religious Life," p. 226.
8. Ibid., p. 224.

his through restraint. The Dionysian man, opening himself up to the mystical even at the risk of madness, stands opposed to the contemplative, whose goals are calm vision. "The problem for the spiritual man, the man seeking perfection, is to curb the sensibility; for the artist, to liberate the sensibility."[9] But the artist too seeks perfection of his gifts.

In his interview with David Kherdian, however, he describes a complex attitude toward perfection in art. As his poetic craft matured until it became something unconscious, he turned to printing so that he might have another craft to develop in. He speaks of approaching facility in a craft, having it become unconscious, but perfection seems more threatening than encouraging as a goal, perhaps because it suggests a *willed* achievement which consciousness controls. He speaks of perfecting the work as an act of *concretizing* or *memorializing* the craft. "You write a perfect poem, a perfect book of poems, and concretize it in a perfect format established on absolutely authentic materials."[10]

He renounces the search for perfection in either printing or poetry, however, arguing that the norms of perfection finally work against themselves and become a demand for *perfectionism.* "To go beyond it is worse, believe me, than to fail to reach it. . . . What is over-done is more than finished, it is finished off, 'finalized'—the thing that has happened to so much modern poetry."[11] Perfectionism is the violation of the tomb, he says, whereas imperfection, "as for instance in the gash, actually liberates the charisma."

The terms "memorialize," "concretize" have to do primarily with finding the right form for what he wants to do or say in art. But form means something more than patterns created by technique here, for facility in the craft only signals an intermediate stage in the artist's development. "The craft has to be memorialized in the flesh, and the flesh has to be memorialized in the spirit, the life principle. Then you are free. . . . She, perfection, delivers you."[12] *Perfection*, *Sophia*, Divine Wisdom, and the Muse become the same figure, the feminine principle, the receptor of the charisma. When he speaks of learning to print, Brother Antoninus speaks of it as having to do with what Jung calls Sensation, the concrete side of experience. He needs first to learn

9. Ibid., p. 225.
10. David Kherdian, *Six Poets of the San Francisco Renaissance* (Fresno, Calif.: Giligia Press, 1966), p. 169.
11. Ibid., p. 139.
12. Ibid., p. 140.

techniques, which means to be straitly confined by them, but only so that at a later point he will have internalized them sufficiently to be free even to violate them. *Form*, whether it derive from a religious commitment, a theological framework, the liturgical year, a schema tracing his conversion through the psychological stages represented by Saint Augustine, Saint Francis, and Saint John of the Cross, or the psychology of Jung, stands over against *technique*. It becomes the synthesis of craft and content for him.

Such an explanation must not be taken to minimize the importance of Antoninus's religious commitment. Whether or not the reader understands why he needs to contain his poems within the frameworks established by the Forewords to his books, there can be no doubt that the poet's need for form, in this larger sense, is so genuine that we could not have the poetry without it. And if a number of poems seem deeply flawed because of the framework, others owe their great success to it.

Quite aside from the influence of a religious vocation on the development of his charismatic side, his need for framework would help explain Brother Antoninus's attraction-repulsion for the institutional life. The institution links a solitary person to others; it provides a conventionalized life-style which balances the undisciplined life of the charismatic; it develops the intellectual and rational faculties to keep pace with the intuition, emotion, and sensation; finally, it is, in his terms, the *active* life, as over against the contemplative life of the artist.

Especially as the institutional life requires that the individual submit his inspirations to the judgment of the collective, represented both by the tradition and the superior, it also provides such a counterweight to the charismatic that when Brother Antoninus speaks of the "creative tension between the point of view of the superior and the point of view of the subject," he says "That tension is the crucifixion." The point of union for the creative artist in the religious life is a cross, he says elsewhere.

In *The Hazards of Holiness* (1962), the stream of poetry which had been choked out in the early years of his religious vocation flows again, for he has taken as theme the spiritual aridity which shut off poetry. Once again the reader is introduced to the poetry through a Foreword which explains it in theological and personal terms. This time the poems are also framed by Jungian psychology.

The Foreword is in two senses an apology for the poetry. Antoninus justifies it as "objectification of inner experience" which he calls "the most efficacious of all acts of relief, except prayer," and he appeals to W. B. Yeats for support: "We gaze not at a work of art, but the re-creation of the man through that art. . . ." From T. S. Eliot he takes the image of the poet as one who writes to exorcise his demons, not to communicate with others. Brother Antoninus offers poems which seek to *objectify*, *concretize*, or *memorialize* his inner experience. His poems represent a victory over himself, and he argues for judging them on that basis.

The second apology seeks to explain away the material from which the poetry comes, for fear that it will seem offensive or blasphemous, especially coming from a Dominican brother. Here he resorts to two explanations, the first an invocation of "that famous Dark Night of the Soul," the second the dream world of depth psychology.

> Against the grain, compounded of the hallucinatory and the obscene, no less than of the transcendental and the sublime, the imagery seeks back against the primordial anguishes, encounters the mute demon and the vocal ghost. . . . [13]

Once again he fights his inner war as a battle to discover a form for his poetry, but once again the form is theological rather than literary. The paired opposites occur again, this time with much greater debt to Jung's psychology, so the tension also exists, but over everything there is the reassurance, *cum permissu Superiorum.*

The Hazards of Holiness has three sections, titled "Friendship and Enmity," "The Dark Face of God," and "Love and Violence." Seven of the poems are introduced by dreams which generated them. A number of others have epigraphs or explanations which link them to the same kind of nonrational source. The dreams are about traveling—on caravan, on pilgrimage, returning for the poet's mother's funeral—and about death. Journeys, darkness, graves and coffins, erotic images and impulses, being swallowed up, dominate the imagery of the dreams.

The relation of freedom and guilt is the theme of both his dream-life and his poetry. "Jacob and the Angel" sets the tone for the entire book. In his dream, the poet is on caravan to the Holy Land but also returning home from exile. He and his guides make camp beside a river,

---

13. Brother Antoninus, *The Hazards of Holiness* (Garden City, N.Y.: Doubleday, 1962), p. 6.

intending to cross over in the morning. He has a dream-within-a-dream that he has come home to his father's house but finds it "deathly vacant"; he wakes to find the caravan gone and the way across the river barred by a tall defender with a rifle. Because he has been used by his guides, who are thieves, the poet is indistinguishable from them and the servant shoots him. As the bullet flies across the distance, "like a meteor from outer space," the poet feels within himself "the whole destiny of the human race in its struggle toward realization, . . . incredibly concretized within my one tormented life-span, and actualized in my very flesh. . . ." As he sinks into the water, the poet tries to communicate to the faithful servant "a gesture of desperate truth" to establish "the authentic character of what is real." He does not know whether he has succeeded, but his final affirmation is that the energies within him have been purged and transformed so that the water can have no final power over this "core of absolute existence."

The poem describes the interconnectedness of liberation and guilt in the Jacob story. Jacob the supplanter is driven into exile because of his mother's fondness, but there he sees "the laddered angels in their intercourse with earth," the liberating sign which frees him "from the mother's death-hug." But then his mother's brother, who tricks him into marrying Leah instead of Rachel, becomes a symbol of guilt. "Deep down the offended father/Lived on symbolic in the maid's evasive sire." Through service to the father-substitute he gains strength to gain the next liberation, receiving another sign of angels that he has become "father-freed." Now he can turn toward home to offer restitution to his brother. Now he meets the angel, whom he mistakes for Esau, and struggles with his twin. This must be both his ultimate restitution and his ultimate liberation; he must both win and lose the battle, for this twin identity is both an angel and Esau's champion.

The poem is very different from the dream. What they have in common is the imagery associated with struggling to cross the stream to confront the defender. The obscure guilt-feelings of the dream, hinted at in images of exile and the vacant family home, ramify in the Jacob myth to include both the poet's parent-child conflict and the theme of fraternal conflict which dominates Genesis. The relationship between dream and poem is such, however, that the latter becomes a Jungian homily on the bible story rather than a re-creation of its meaning.

> One queasy crime—and the score-long exiled years!
> How many mockeries of the inscrutable archetypes
> Must we endure to meet our integration?
> Is it fate or merely malice that has made
> Us overreach our brother in the burdened womb?

The struggle with the angel becomes a symbol of political development and the integration of the personality as aspects of one another. As "the night-wombed nations murmur into birth" while the wrestling match goes on, Jacob's wives, "twin aspects of his dark divided life" huddle in the dark and pray for the outcome. He wins his final liberation, a blessing from the angel, "who seized/In the heart's black hole the angel of intellection," and receives his new name, "Israel, striver with God." Now he can go to his reconciliation with his brother, who recognizes his new nature.

As always, Brother Antoninus is at his best when handling violent language and physical sensation and at his weakest when he makes his fable serve a doctrine. That the doctrine in this case is about the integration of personality makes no difference; it is intrusive on the fable and awkward when poeticized. Nothing in the events in the poem prepares us for the explanation of the struggle with the angel as the calling up of intellection from the unconscious, represented by the "heart's black hole." The language of the poem becomes abstract and sermonic when the theme needs to be explored through physical imagery. The questions are rhetorical in the worst sense—they are neither taken seriously as requests for information nor open enough to make the answers interesting to us.

A number of the poems show the same difficulty of reconciling the discursive and nondiscursive. "Saints," for example, is built up of short, choppy lines which convey the emotion through explosives and harsh monosyllables. But the discourse is all orthodoxy.

> Not even God
> Has power to force an evil act
> But man does!

And the reader cannot respond to the emotional tension, no matter how genuine he believes it, in such a line as "God? Saints? Faith? Rapture? Vision? Dream?—/Where?" "The Word" is an example of the most abstract discourse broken up into short lines and made into a kind of shorthand to give the impression of poetry. No physical imagery, no metaphor or simile borrowed from the senses appears in the poem; the reader has nothing to draw him into the poem except the argument, which is as obscure as it is abstract. The poem begins:

> One deepness,
> That mammoth inchoation,
> Nothingness freighted on its term of void,
> Oblivion abandoned to its selflessness,
> Aching for a clue.

Once more we recognize the energy in the verbals, but they do not take us anywhere. The Word was made flesh and dwelt among us precisely so it need not be so abstract and unavailable to human understanding and perception. Here the senses are utterly starved. What the poem says of the Word would baffle the most severe Platonist. Where he has a metaphor by which he can develop the inner struggle with God, Brother Antoninus can make his craft work for him. "In the Breach," for example, speaks of God as both the killer and the midwife. The reluctance of the child to leave the womb and its compulsion to do so, for the sake of life, work together in his elaboration of the images of birth.

In "A Frost Lay White on California," a dream of finding a raped dead woman and realizing that he had committed the crime stimulates a poem in which the poet engages in a colloquy with God throughout the frozen night. The figures of the woman and the dog, which appear in the dream, become images by which God describes His relationship to the poet. Stanzas alternate in which God speaks and the poet reflects on his inner state and links it to the cold darkness around him, but the power of the poem comes through the poet's reflections, for the begging of God seems diffuse and elaborate—too much what we might imagine ourselves giving Him to say in a dialogue we wrote. "I am your image."

> *Close your eyes now and be what I am.*
> *Which is—yourself!*
> *The you who am I!*

Operating underneath this inner dialogue, however, is something akin to Coleridge's "silent ministry" of frost. The rain which has been threatening all through the hours of the poet's vigil, comes with the dawn, "a slow spilth of deliverance," breaking up the frost. ". . . it was falling, I knew, out of the terrifying helplessness of God." The poem works because it relies ultimately on natural imagery and the feel of human experience to convey what is happening spiritually, rather than giving us arguments for, or opinions about, the mercy of God.

Brother Antoninus wishes to use his poetry to gain victories over himself, but the best poems, and perhaps the surest victories, are those like "In All These Acts" and "God Germed in Raw Granite," where he focuses his attention on describing the goings-on of nature with all the precise detail he can achieve. Here he might be said to follow the example of Gerard Manley Hopkins, whose finest nature poems grow out of the discovery, *in the scene*, that the Holy Ghost works through it, and whose finest poems about people grow from his discovery that Christ is in each of them. "In All These Acts" chronicles with horrified fascination a wind storm in the forest which tosses logs in "staggering gyrations of splintered kindling." An elk, caught between two crashing logs, is torn open and dies in spasms of agony:

> Arched belly-up and died, the snapped spine
> Half torn out of his peeled back, his hind legs
> Jerking that gasped convulsion, the kick of spasmed life,
> Paunch plowed open, purple entrails
> Disgorged from the basketwork ribs
> Erupting out, splashed sideways, wrapping him
> Gouted in blood, flecked with the brittle sliver of bone.

Vigorous verbs and verbal adjectives, explosive monosyllables, tight linking of words through alliteration and inner rhyme, bring the scene before us in overpowering fashion. But the scene does not stand alone; it parallels the river's violent "frenzy of capitulation" as it destroys itself in "the mother sea." And in a counter movement, the poet describes the salmon leaving the sea about to make their way to the place they were born, to "beat that barbarous beauty out" in their urge to spawn. The elk's death-throes, the river's self-destruction to feed the sea, the salmon's immolation-propagation become symbols of

> . . . the wakeful, vengeful beauty,
> Devolving itself of its whole constraint,
> Erupting as it goes.

The poet sees the ambiguities suggested by *wakeful, vengeful beauty*, implied by the constellation of violence and sex, and he affirms them, seeing Christ in them, "the modes of His forth-showing,/His serene agonization." This is as theologically orthodox as any poem Brother

Antoninus has written, but here we believe the insight to have come from the poem itself. Christ does not stand over against this violence; He is not escape from the world of nature or compensation for it. "In all these acts/Christ crouches and seethes." He is the way things are; and fascination with the barbarous beauty expended for the continuation of the race finally turns to affirmation of Him.

What makes the poem effective is suggested by the phrase "These are the modes of His forth-showing." The poet argues his poem *in* the images, and their larger significance arises from this unsentimental look at what they are. To use one of the simplest critical distinctions, the poem has *shown* us, rather than telling us.

Similarly, "God Germed in Raw Granite" shows us through images the emergence of outward shape from inner nature. Word choice and length of line distinctively shape a poem whose theme is shape. Freedom and constraint, expressive form, the tug of paired opposites—all these preoccupations of the poet's life as artist and religious enter the poem through his description of rock, that most fixed and static aspect of the creation. He sees into its source, its germ, "the tortured/Free-flow of lava, the igneous/Instant of conception." The germ is feminine, "Woman within!" and the love of man for woman partakes of the desire for inner coherence and the desire for God.

> In the blind heart's core, when we,
> Well-wedded merge, by Him
> Twained into one and solved there,
> Are these still three? Are three
> So oned, in the full-forthing . . . ?

Theological commitments influence it—e.g., the doctrine of the trinity and the conception of marriage as a type of Christ's love for the Church—but nothing occurs in the poem *because* a doctrine exists to cover such a situation. The wonder of sexual love generates the meditation on the mystery that two can become simultaneously one and three; it requires no explicit reference to liturgy or scripture, no allegorizing of the Song of Songs. We go back to the experience which was the source of the allegory and realize afresh why human love symbolizes the divine.

The Hazards of Holiness is a flawed but powerful book. The flaws seem greatest where the poet cannot let experiences—dreams, temptations, sins, insights—stand by themselves and make their own meanings.

The allegorizing spirit lets things stand for other things too easily, especially when a Dominican brother is publishing *cum permissu.*

Brother Antoninus acknowledges that the religious artist also struggles with the inner censor, which may tell him that words and attitudes are unacceptable coming from him. Those elements in his poetry which make for the reader's dissatisfaction even in the most vigorous, deeply felt and sincere poems, carry the *cum permissu* stamp on them. The retelling of biblical stories—even the bloody tales of John the Baptist and Judith and Holofernes, where his warrant for speaking of sexual enticement is clear—the meditations on saints, the canticles, have been hedged round by explanations from the inner censor. Perhaps the clearest example is "The Song the Body Dreamed in the Spirit's Mad Behest," where the title, an epigraph from the Canticle of Canticles, and a gloss on the Imagination introduce the poem in such a way as to neutralize any shock caused by the explicitly sexual imagery.

Speaking of prayer, Martin Buber describes the tension between spontaneity and the subjectivized reflection which assails it. "The assailant is consciousness, the overconsciousness of this man here that he is praying, that he is *praying*, that *he* is praying."[14] A similar overconsciousness seems to operate in Brother Antoninus's poetry: he writes to objectify inner experience and to gain release from inner torment, but he also writes to instruct, to give *exempla* acceptable to his readers, his superiors, but primarily to that inner assailant which tells him *he* is writing a poem.

Not uncommonly, the worst poems written by an able poet fail not because of a change in subject matter or a change in technique but because they miss the fragile balance between extremes which he accomplishes in his best work. The characteristic techniques and attitudes, the diction and imagery, remain, but reduced to stock response. All the tensions which have shaped Brother Antoninus's poetry stand most starkly opposed in his latest book, *The Rose of Solitude* (1967), but now, under the pressure of his subject or of his obligation to make something affirmatively Christian of it, his poems express the worst emotional excesses and technical gaucheries of which he is capable. He calls the book a love-poem sequence and tells us it is an interior monologue continuing from "In Savage Wastes," which concluded *The Haz-*

14. Will Herberg, ed., *The Writings of Martin Buber* (New York: Meridian Books, 1956), p. 110.

ards of Holiness. That poem tells of a monk who returns to the world when a dream shows him that he has not escaped its temptations by fleeing to the desert. His "travail of self-enlightenment" continued in *The Rose of Solitude.*

Behind the poems is a love affair between a monk and a divorced woman, a dancer. When a situation which must not be, *is*, the suffering is intense. Two kinds of fidelity clash, for each is good and bears the stamp of the divine, yet they are inimical to one another. Breaking the vows is sin, but renouncing the human love is not virtuous; something lies deeper in this conflict which must be worked through for the sake of a more profound understanding of faithfulness.

> The man of God and the woman of the world are, from the point of view of the normative consciousness, polar opposites. But like all polar opposites they are drawn together by an ineluctable attraction and mutual fascination, verifying their distinctness each on the other's being. . . . When these inner realities emerge and move together, what happens is an expansion of awareness beyond the code of manners that society has established for either, and a profound crisis in the moral life of two people. [15]

As this passage indicates, two kinds of doctrines will need to find expression and resolution in the poetry, orthodox Catholic theology and Jungian psychology. The handling of dreams in *The Hazards of Holiness* and the interview with David Kherdian would have prepared us for the Jungian emphasis. We can expect, therefore, as the Foreword emphasizes, that the masculine-feminine dichotomy will operate on many levels and that a great deal of attention will be given to archetypal figures, images, and relationships.

These ways of ordering experience to comprehend it result in two kinds of poetry in *The Rose of Solitude*: long poem-sequences made up of terse stanzas which are closer to entries in a spiritual diary than they are to lyrics; and long canticles exploiting a long line and loose verse-paragraph in a fashion "half rationale and half celebration." The characteristic weaknesses of each are evident in the book.

Part One of the book, "I Nail My Life," made up of three poem-sequences, gives us the data of the relationship. This is the spiritual diary, a documentary account of a developing relationship and the

15. Brother Antoninus, "Foreword" to *The Rose of Solitude* (Garden City, N.Y.: Doubleday, 1967), pp. x—xi.

poet's attempt to put it in context. The separate poems are made up of the simplest subject-verb sentences put together in the simplest parallels. While the first poems, in "The Way of Life and the Way of Death," give us the sensual accompaniments of the relationships, the woman's signatures—poinsettias, the flesh of mangoes and guaves, rum—the later ones become increasingly sparse and vacant of sensory imagery.

The canticle form calls for a rich sensual fabric, the piling up of colors, sounds and tastes and luxuriating in them for their association with the loved one. Liturgies derived from the Song of Songs celebrate Mary in the language of a lover. The form tends toward shapelessness and emotional sprawl, however, since it develops out of the loose parallelism of Hebraic poetry and has no necessary conclusion or rounding off. "The Canticle of the Rose" joins emotional sprawl to theological abstraction, asserting as doctrine about the woman he loves what we could, at best, grant only as an extravagant expression of one's personal feelings. As a consequence, we withhold our assent from both the theological and the personal assertions.

> And if I call you great, and if I call you holy, and if I
>> say that even your sins enforce the sheer reality of what you are,
> Know that I speak because in you I gaze on Him, by you I see
>> Him breathe, and in your flesh I clasp Him to my breast.

From the first poems, the speaker claims to recognize something redemptive in this relationship; he calls it both *necessitum peccatum* and *felix culpa*. The woman becomes a type of Christ, a symbol of divine love, a bearer of grace to be identified through the image of the Rose with the Mother of God. If we are to take all this as unambiguously true, we must then ask what the issue of the book is. Surely the torment of breaking vows must disappear in the light of such a revelation. If that is too simpleminded an approach to take, are we to read the book as we would read other interior monologues—as an account of spiritual development from confusion to clarity, from self-deception to honesty? Such a stance would demand of us a certain ironic detachment and awareness of moral and intellectual ambiguities when the speaker makes extravagant claims for the woman he loves. Nothing in either the poetry or the Foreword, however, indicates that the poet wishes us to take the book at anything other than face value.

"My art can err only in insufficiency, my fierce excesses crack on the ineluctable reality of what you are," he insists. To take him seriously on his own terms, therefore, means to indict him for inflating his subject beyond credibility. The poignancy of his forbidden love for a beautiful woman gets lost in the extravagance of his claims for it; she becomes a symbol of divine love the same way the bullfrog became a bull. We might say of the poetry that it has the meaning but missed the experience; events are so rapidly turned into their significance that we lose the feel and texture of experience itself, despite Brother Antoninus's lifelong preoccupation as a poet with the-blunt, harsh work, the vigorous verb. Here every noun has its Latinate-sounding adjective, lines and phrases are strung out to. prolong a mood of hectic excitement. Striving for the vatic, the poem achieves only the bathetic.

> I have said before:
> All the destinies of the divine
> In her converge.

What creates difficulties in the canticle form operates in the simple poem-sequences as well. Clearly the poet wants to make her a symbol of many things having to do with the opening up of his spiritual life, but once again he runs into difficulties because the psychological-theological form he accepts demands that she be pure archetype. Symbols are built up by slow accretion—the history of the rose in Western literature illustrates the point—not by appropriation. The woman the poet loves does not *participate* in the reality she points to; the middle ground between tenor and vehicle of a metaphor does not exist.

There are poems and passages from poems in *The Rose of Solitude* which move us by their spiritual perception and poetic tact; when the balance is struck, the poetry is effective in Brother Antoninus's characteristic ways. And even when the reader feels obliged to find greatest fault with the poetry, there is never any doubt of the poet's intense sincerity or that he has suffered through everything he writes about. If his poetry achieves the victory over himself that he wishes, we must be grateful for that, and wish him well. But if we bring to our reading the expectation that form and content support each other in such a way that poetic problems are solved poetically and not doctrinally, we must remain dissatisfied with much of Brother Antoninus's work. The inner censor, whether operating from the standpoint of Catholic doctrine or

Jungian psychology, closes too many ways to Brother Antoninus; the overconsciousness that tells him he is *writing* imposes too heavy a burden on his work—and perhaps on the man as well. Externally imposed form, which accompanies the *cum permissu* stamp, wrestles with the material of his life as the angel wrestles Jacob in his poem, with equally unclear results. Among the chief hazards of holiness for him seems to be the incapacity to be free as a poet. His tragedy may be that there can be no final victories in his inner war except at the cost of his poetry.

6.

A Poetry of
Exploration

In her "Statement on Poetics" in 1959 Denise Levertov wrote:

> I believe poets are instruments on which the power of poetry plays. But they are also makers, craftsmen: It is given to the seer to see, but it is then his responsibility to communicate what he sees, that they who cannot see may see, since we are "members one of another."

A poem is a living thing, not merely by courtesy of metaphor, but literally. And it is a mystery not to be solved but to be approached reverently, meditated upon, and affirmed. Both her critical writing and her poetry insist on such an approach to poetry and, behind it, to life. Poems should evidence an "inner harmony" which is in "utter contrast to the chaos" of life, but not a manufactured harmony or a fantasy compensation for the way things really are. "For me, back of the idea of organic form is the concept that there is a form in all things (and in our experience) which the poet can discover and reveal."[1] As the lines from "The Artist" put it, "The true artist: capable, practicing skillful;/ maintains dialogue with his heart, meets things with his mind." The act of writing poetry is first an act of opening oneself to experience in such a way that its *inscape* becomes revealed to us.

As her critical writings testify, the language of mystery—though not mystification—most appropriately expresses how poems are "given" to and received by the poet. Sense experiences, memories, the unconscious, some image or word come together, constellate for the poet. In

1. Denise Levertov, "Some Notes on Organic Form," *New Directions* 20 (1968): 123–28.

order to *have* or *grasp* and *interpret* this complex of experiences, the poet must discover some "expressive and unifying act," some form, "an inscape that relates the apparently unrelated." This he does through meditation and contemplation, opening up to or centering down upon this constellation of elements. Denise Levertov deliberately uses words from the religious vocabulary and acknowledges their source. "The act of art evokes a spirit, and in assuming the existence of a spirit, and the possibility of a transformation by means of that spirit, it is an act of prayer. It is a testimony of that *participation mystique*, that involvement of the individual in a life beyond himself, which is a basic element of religion in the broadest and deepest sense." [2]

The poet "muses," which she defines literally as standing open-mouthed, waiting for "inspiration." As things fall together into a pattern, a correspondence between those things and words occurs. The poet is "brought to speech." "Correspondence," "counterparts," "analogies," "resemblances," "natural allegories," are all words which Denise Levertov uses to speak of poetic forms in relation to reality. "Such a poetry is exploratory."

> All trivial parts of
> world-about-us speak in the forms
> of themselves and their counterparts!
>
> ("A Straw Swan at Christmas")

General discussions of methods of poetic composition are notoriously unhelpful when used to gloss particular poems, and this would be especially true for Denise Levertov's poetry, for she is telling us neither "how-to-write-an-organic-poem" nor even "how-I-write." Discourse cannot teach us how to intuit, but we may catch from her tone and attitude in her critical writings some ways in which our reading may be exploratory, as her poetry is. A good test case is her poem "Illustrious Ancestors," from *Overland to the Islands* (1958).

> The Rav
> of Northern White Russia declined,
> in his youth, to learn the
> language of birds, because
> the extraneous did not interest him; nevertheless
> when he grew old it was found

2. Denise Levertov, "Asking the Fact for the Form," mimeographed lecture (Wabash College, December 6, 1962).

he understood them anyway, having
listened well, and as it is said, "prayed
      with the bench and the floor." He used
what was at hand—as did
Angel Jones of Mold, whose meditations
were sewn into coats and britches.
      Well, I would like to make,
thinking some line still taut between me and them,
poems direct as what the birds said,
hard as a floor, sound as a bench,
mysterious as the silence when the tailor
would pause with his needle in the air.

The poem opens with an artless telling of a family tale. If we are used to looking to the ends of lines for strong words or active verbs to carry the energy of the poem, we are disappointed: "the," "because," "nevertheless," do not drive us forward. The flat tone and matter-of-fact handling of details seem, in fact, to undercut the promise of the title. But the anecdote engages us deeply, for it resonates like a good Hasidic tale. The words and details invite meditation by their very simplicity and artlessness. For what strikes us first is that the miraculous itself is being treated matter-of-factly. And from that simple contrast others become clear: youth and age, ignorance and wisdom, the extraneous and what lies at hand. The Rav, caught up in one understanding of the spiritual life in his youth, declines to learn what is extraneous, the language of the birds. But in his old age, because he attended to the unmysterious and everyday disciplines of Hasidism, that other capacity has come as an additional gift. The implications of the tale are rich. On the one hand, there might be the danger of pride in the Rav's decision that the language of the birds was uninteresting and extraneous; but he may also have avoided a temptation to greater pride in the piling up of *power*. In refusing to study what is a secret to man, he skirts the temptations of the magical—often associated with the demonic in Martin Buber's *Tales of the Hasidim* and his historical chronicle *For the Sake of Heaven.* The Rav did not focus on achieving powers, but on "listening well" and "praying *with*" the tools and furniture of his workaday life, "He used what was at hand." Because he had ears, he heard, as Jesus' parable in the Gospel of Mark puts it; because he learned how to listen well, he discovered in the wisdom of old age that nothing is extraneous.

The Hasidic tale of the Rav could be complete in itself, but this poem concerns inheritance and keeping faith with one's gifts, so the poet tells about an ancestor from the other side of the family and another tradition. Angel Jones also used what was at hand in such a way as to spiritualize its nature. We know of him only that he *sewed* his meditations into everyday garments, "Coats and britches." The matter-of-fact becomes a bearer of the miraculous without ceasing to preserve its original nature. Both ancestors were *makers*, and the poet affirms that some line is "still taut between me and them." She meditates on them, as they did on what was around them, and discovers what kind of poems she wants to make. Here she gathers up the threads which have run through the poem and weaves them together into the fabric she wants for her poems: concretion, precision, and through them the mysterious and the silent.

Such a reading of the poem seems to rest primarily on the idea-content, but what has made the ideas available to us, and filled them with their peculiar value, has much more to do with tone and rhythm, the movement along that taut line which connects the illustrious ancestors to the poet and the poet to the reader, than with the ideas themselves.

The poem does not call attention to itself; but its quiet stateliness leads us to those qualities of directness, hardness, and soundness, and finally to the suspension at the end of the poem, the slowing down which leaves us silent and still in the presence of mystery. The poem is like the ancestors, ordinary and yet illustrious, filled with light.

Both the subject matter and the treatment of "Illustrious Ancestors" lead a critic to ask what values of Hasidism have affected Denise Levertov's poetry. *The Jacob's Ladder* is introduced by one of the *Tales of the Hasidim: Later Masters* which throws light on both the form of that book and on all her poetry. Rabbi Moshe of Kobryn, meditating on the story of Jacob's ladder, sees Jacob as everyman. The ladder stands on the earth but reaches the heavens; man is one of countless shards of clay, but his soul reaches to heaven. " 'And behold the angels of God ascending and descending on it'—even the ascent and descent of the angels depend on my deeds."

We may note, first of all, that the particular way Rabbi Moshe breaks open the story tells us a great deal. He speaks out of the tradition of exegesis found in the Talmud—text and commentary on it which combines the most profound respect for every word with the greatest freedom for the imagination to play on the text. The rabbi, like the artist, "maintains dialogue with his heart, meets things with his mind." Jacob and what befell him is history, but it is also allegory; it has meaning in itself and in the correspondences it reveals in all human lives. Behind this exegetical method is a specific anthropology, expressed by Denise Levertov in Saint Paul's words from the Epistle to the Romans, "we are members one of another." One finds in Hasidism a deep-rooted humanism and ethical concern. One also finds an equally deep-rooted respect for the creation, this world, as an abode of holiness. Another tale of Rabbi Moshe of Kobryn, which immediately follows the one quoted in *The Jacob's Ladder*, in *Tales of the Hasidim: Later Masters*, brings all these elements together:

> The rabbi of Kobryn taught:
> God says to man, as he said to Moses: "Put off thy shoes from thy feet"—put off the habitual which encloses your foot, and you will know that the place on which you are now standing is holy ground. For there is no rung of human life on which we cannot find the holiness of God everywhere and at all times. [3]

One *puts off* the habitual but does not repudiate it; when the habitual is seen afresh, it testifies to the holy. Such a view worked out in the writing of poetry necessarily carries with it a distinct perception of the role of the poet. He can be neither the seer nor the maker as those two models have been understood by many poets since the Romantic movement; the poet is neither God who makes all things nor Adam who names all things. He is not the rebel or outcast defying God and making a contemptuous, magical fantasy world. If we do not become too enamored of the image, we might say that the poet is like Jacob in Rabbi Moshe's tale, who sees *in a dream* the ladder between heaven and earth, who puts off the habitual and perceives the holy, and for whom seeing carries an imperative to act.

One would expect, from Denise Levertov's affinities for other poets and for her illustrious ancestors, that her poetry would be marked by delight in shapes and textures, strange, evocative words, clearly delineated scenes. She is always interested by *inwardness*, what gives meaning to shape, texture, and scene, but much of the music of her poetry comes from her delight in the details of things themselves.

The religious response to a mystery is celebration, not explanation. At her best, Denise Levertov communicates both the holiness in a scene

3. Martin Buber, *Tales of the Hasidim: Later Masters*, trans. Olga Marx (New York: Schocken Books, 1947–48), p. 170.

and the "greeting of the spirit," in John Keats's phrase, which makes it real to man. "She has no superior in this clarification of a scene," says Robert Duncan, ". . . that crossing of the inner and the outer reality, where we have our wholeness of feeling in the universe."

If her poetry has its typical excellences, it has its typical weaknesses, as well. A number of the early poems fail to engage our deeper interest precisely because they assert what they do not persuade us of—a meaningful correspondence between scene and an inner reality. One person's celebration can be another's dull party, after all; and though the capacity to celebrate is valuable, it does not necessarily lead to a broader range of experience or insight. Where the poems fail, they do so typically for one of two reasons: they inflate or sentimentalize an experience, or they grasp for counterparts too hastily and produce false analogies.

No method of meditation can guarantee success, and a poetry of exploration must be valued for the quality of its exploring, not merely for its success in finding, but there are inherent problems in Denise Levertov's poetic method. To wish poems to be a counterforce, to have an inner harmony "in utter contrast to the chaos in which they exist," can lead to filtering out too much of the chaos too soon. Musing, meditating, recollecting emotion in tranquillity—which is a particular form of poetic meditation—can flatten out the highs and lows of a life and produce " 'common speech'/ a dead level," in place of poetry. Those who have practiced the art of meditation testify how hard it is to break away from familiar ideas and stock responses; the tendency is to graft the new onto the familiar, rather than to launch forward into the threatening and the unexpected.

In "Notes of a Scale" Denise Levertov refers to one of the *Tales of the Hasidim: The Early Masters*, which might serve as a gloss on her poetry. Rabbi Elimelekh distinguishes between two kinds of wonders, those produced by magicians as illusions to surprise others, and those he calls wonders "from the true world" which God enables one to perform. The latter take the performer by surprise—they are given, not learned.

> 'A wonder
> from the true world,'
> he who accomplished it
> 'overwhelmed with the wonder
> which arises out of his doing,'. . .

THE INNER WAR

Magic is a learned skill, which depends on drawing from one's stock with facility. The true wonders come when the learned response, the stereotypes, the methods of meditation are broken open. One may also distinguish two kinds of poems in the same way. The first rests almost entirely on the associative process taking place in the poet's mind.

The second kind of poem, the true wonder, must be difficult to describe or it would not be what it is. Some common characteristics may be suggested, however, The darker side of experience and the unconscious have more play. Things go more deeply into the poet. The poem proceeds both associatively and dialogically, in Buber's sense. Things are *themselves* first, with their own clarity and individuality; they do not lose their natures in a divine All or gain value because we perceive their symbolic meaning. Buber insists, when he speaks of the *I-Thou* relationship, that it be called *meeting* or *witnessing*. We are addressed and we answer. He speaks of the "complete relational event" which is knowing the *Thou*. ". . . No 'going beyond sense-experience' is necessary; for every experience, even the most spiritual, would yield us only an *It*. Nor is any recourse necessary to a world of ideas and values, for they cannot become presentness to us." [4]

> From the shrivelling gray
> silk of its cocoon
> a creature slowly
>   is pushing out
> to stand clear—
>
>> not a butterfly,
>>   petal that floats at will across
>>   the summer breeze
>>
>> not a furred
>> moth of the night
>>   crusted with indecipherable
>>   gold—
>
> some primal-shaped, plain-winged, day-flying thing.

Nothing has to be said of the relational event; it requires no predicate. It need not suggest counterparts or archetypes to speak to us. This event, rightly called "The Disclosure," stands in its own radiance, and to attach qualities to it, even the quality of holiness, would lessen its value. We know someone observes what is happening, but the percep-

---

4. Martin Buber, *I and Thou*, trans. Ronald Gregor Smith (New York: Charles Scribner's Sons, 1954), p. 77.

tions pursue the *via negativa*, "not a butterfly, . . . not a furred moth," until the "thing" stands clear as itself. It does not come for naming; in fact the poet never gains even that degree of power over it which comes with knowing something's name.

Louis Martz, speaking of the meditative poem in English, says that it records the creation of ". . . a self that is, ideally, one with itself, with other human beings, with created nature, and with the supernatural." [5] The typical meditative poem begins with the fact of separation, at least the distinction of subject and object, and by processes of association, memory, imagination, and "conversation" between subject and object, it creates that self which is at one with itself and everything not-itself.

But there is another kind of meditation, found in the poetry of Robert Bly, James Wright, and Gary Snyder as well as in Denise Levertov, where the discovery or creation of the self is unimportant, and only *seeing* matters.

> Zaddik, you showed me
> the Stations of the Cross
>
> and I saw
> not what the almost abstract
>
> tiles held—world upon world—
> but at least
>
> a shadow of what
> might be seen there if mind and heart
>
> gave themselves to meditation,
> deeper
>
> and deeper into Imagination's
> holy forest. . . .

> ("Letter to William Kintner")

The three books, *With Eyes at the Back of Our Heads*, *The Jacob's Ladder*, and *O Taste and See*, impress us with her serene delight in the world and pleasure in making poems which celebrate the world, "all that lives/to the imagination's tongue."

In the presence of so much which is good, one feels misanthropic to complain at what is lacking, but the poems are weakened from lack of a serious treatment of evil. The world in which "doubleness," suffering,

5. Louis L. Martz, *The Poetry of Meditation* (New Haven: Yale University Press, 1954), p. 322.

and evil must be fought, if only to a draw, every day, is not taken very seriously in the poems.

Evil has no existence in itself but is only good "in abeyance," apparently. In "The Necessity" she takes the Hasidic image of the divine sparks encased in all things waiting for the *Teshuvah*, man's act of repentance which sets in motion God's redemption of His creation. But she uses this image to describe the making of poetry.

> each part
> of speech a spark
> awaiting redemption, each
> a virtue, a power
>
> in abeyance unless we
> give it care
> our need designs in us. Then
> all we have led away returns to us.

Even "During the Eichmann Trial," from *The Jacob's Ladder*, and "A March," from *O Taste and See*, two poems which take their subjects directly from contemporary social issues, both center on the appropriate inner response to the issue rather than on arguing a course of action.

Not until *The Sorrow Dance* (1967) and *Relearning the Alphabet* (1970) does she pursue the vision of evil any farther. With *The Sorrow Dance* she has broadened and deepened the range of her poetry to correspond to the degree of involvement she now has in social concerns. The dominant tone in the book is grief; not just in the larger occasions for grief, the death of the poet's older sister and the war in Vietnam, but even in the poems rejoicing in the natural world, where joy and the awareness of mortality support one another. In place of what Ralph Mills, Jr. called "poetry of the Immediate," we find poetry of the absent, of the hard-won insight or confirmation. The poetry is characterized by reassessment of the past and a reaching after new experiences in order to consolidate them within the self.

In grieving we prolong the pain of loss by *recollecting* both what gave us joy and what made us guilty in the relationship. The process is analogous to artistic creation in that memory and imagination work together to apprehend the significant form which makes available to us the ongoing meaning of a life or a cluster of events. Recollection leads on to incorporation of the other, forgiven and forgiving, into ourselves, and we take up life again, strengthened by the virtues and spirit of

those we have lost. The whole dynamic is beautifully imaged in Denise
Levertov's phrase, "The Sorrow Dance."

"The Wings" strikes the dominant note immediately. Something
"heavy," "black," hangs hidden from view on the speaker's back. "I
can't see it, can't move it." Is it "pure energy I store" or "black/inimi-
cal power, cold"? Is it to be identified with "terror, stupidity/of cold
rage" or is it black only because it is pent up? The very simplest
contrasts begin to bear complex implications. "Black" and its echo or
rhyme words play off against "white," "flight," and "light." Similarly,
"humped and heavy" plays off against "a fountain of light," "the
power of flight." But potency must always be ambiguous.

> could I go
> on one wing,
>
> the white one?

The poems abide in the ambiguity of potency. They trace its dark
roots and speak of the testing which so often precedes the receiving of
new power: emptiness, incapacity, frustration, and incoherence. The
poet recognizes in "The Mutes" that the groans of lust a woman hears
from men in the subway are "grief-language," "language stricken, sickened, cast down/in decrepitude." They are sounds of impotence, but
they translate into other languages—into a wordless tribute to her grace,
into a changed pace, into understanding of life around her. She feels
their truth on her pulse; the sounds of impotence become sounds of
power as the subway train comes echoing through the tunnel to jar to a
halt,

> . . . while her understanding

> keeps on translating:
> 'life after life after life goes by
>
> without poetry,
> without seemliness,
> without love.'

In *O Taste and See* her metaphor for the artist was the All-Day Bird,
"striving/in hope and/good faith to make his notes/ever more precise."
Now it is the earthworm, "out of soil by passage/of himself/construc-
ting/castles of metaphor!" Whereas the All-Day Bird sang full-heartedly
of "Sun/light./Light/light light light," the worm "throws off" his artifacts by contracting and expanding the "muscle of his being." The

images speak of hard labor, being closed in, tilling oneself, but not for the purpose of making art. The artifacts are thrown off as a by-product of the real work, which is aerating "the ground of his living." The artist humbly makes his soul, brings vitality to the ground of living—which sounds so close to Tillich's "ground of being"—and becomes a completed self.

Descent and ascent, from the periphery to the center and out again, renewed—the patterns of the elegy shape "The Sorrow Dance." From generalized despair, the perception of formlessness and incoherence, we move to the particular cause of grief and guilt memorialized in the "Olga Poems," which are the heart of the book. Through grief, the opening up to sorrow, the return from emotional death, we reach a provisional affirmation, the beginnings of new strength. The poet recognizes the world of "The Mutes," where language is "stricken, sickened." In "The Whisper" is a world of terror "filling up fast with/unintelligible signs, . . . arhythmic." Only after the self has been reconstituted by internalizing or incorporating the object of grief within itself, confirming the worthiness of this grief, can the poet recognize that "The Closed World" was the inner world. She quotes from Blake, "If the Perceptive Organs close, their Objects seem to close also."

"Incorporation" or internalization requires facing the threatening *otherness*, the shadow side of one's existence represented by the characteristics of another person, particularly one with whom there has been an unhealed breach. In "A Lamentation" the poet translates all her sister's negative qualities into her own betrayals and denials. She has denied all grief, at the cost of the vitality of love: "Grief dismissed,/and Eros along with grief."

> That robe or tunic, black gauze
> over black and silver my sister wore
> to dance *Sorrow,* hung so long
> in my closet. I have never tried it on.
>   And my dance
> was *Summer*—

To dance *Summer* betrayed her "autumn birthright" in order to please others. Sorrow always characterized Olga; denial of sorrow characterized herself, she now believes. She has betrayed not only her sister—the kind of betrayal the "easy" child feels for profiting by the sibling's difficulties—but she has betrayed her own nature as well.

She has lost definition, as has her world. "Pink sunstripes," "spaces of blue timidly steady" are her colors, not black and silver, the emblems and plumes of her sister. "There are hidden corners of sky/choked with the swept shreds, with pain and ashes." The poem achieves no resolution, but the process of opening up has begun. Blackness, darkness, shadow contend with pink and blue. Sentence fragments image the disconnectedness of her experience, the devaluing of the "I" which should be their subject.

The method of the "Olga Poems" is recollection, the calling back together of a person now "bones and tatters of flesh in earth." To recollect is also to comprehend—to grasp, to assemble in coherent form. Naturally enough, what we did not comprehend in the living person will engage us most in recollecting him. The "Olga Poems" explore the differences between the sisters, from the differences in age and physical maturation to the deep spiritual breaks between them. Olga is always the dark one, both physically and spiritually. At nine she was swept with rage and shame at seeing a slum; where her sister at the same age sees "pride in the whitened doorsteps." At an early age, "*Everything flows*," the Heraclitean doctrine, strikes her consciousness as a counsel of despair. Her sister links the phrase to the hymn "O God, Our Help in Ages Past," "*Time/like an everlasting stream/bears all its sons away*." She therefore puts it in the context of Christian hope.

The contrasts begin to stand clear. Olga never perceives order in her life or in the world, but she longs to impose it. She wants "to browbeat/the poor into joy's/socialist republic," to label the disorder on her desk, base her verses on Keble's *Christian Year*, "To change,/to change the course of the river!"

> But dread
> was in her, a bloodbeat, it was against the rolling dark
> oncoming river she raised bulwarks, . . .

Energy and will characterize Olga, as her sister recalls her; she pits her strength *against* the flow. "What rage for order/disordered her pilgrimage." Olga is a pilgrim—a seeker after holiness—but also a "Black one, incubus," unable to be led along a peaceful path. The tension between these two makes her the cause of disaster to herself and others, "disasters bred of love."

The poet, the easy child, who trusted order and flow, must salvage

from her sister's life some principle to give it meaning. She finds it in
the "candle of compassion" which shone through the darkness.

> Black one, black one,
> there was a white
> candle in your heart.

"That kind candle" alone remains when the "comet's tail" of hatred,
the disasters, even history had "burned down." A definition of Olga's
life grows out of the images of natural force—the flame and the river—
associated with her. They can represent meaningless flux—the disorder
which Olga feared—but they can also image pattern, a cycle of fulfillment in which life and death have deeper meaning. Retracing her sister's life is more than an act of reconciliation, for Olga has not only
been an *opposite* to come to terms with, she has also been a forerunner.
Accordingly, she is example and warning. Since we must all trace some
of the same steps through life to death, what must be learned is in what
spirit to make the trip.

Only when we have internalized the values, or come to terms with
the threats, which the loved one represented to us, can we pronounce a
final benediction over him. So, in the "Olga Poems" Denise Levertov
opens herself to the painful and fragmentary memories until they begin
to cohere around a few images and impressions: the pilgrim, the river
and the sea, the "everlasting arms," the candle, music. These she gathers
up for a final re-creation of her sister's life and an affirmation of its
continuing value for her. Finally, the poet remembers her sister's eyes,
and the effect is as if she looks her fully in the face for the first time.

> Your eyes were the brown gold of pebbles under water.
> I never crossed the bridge over the Roding, dividing
> the open field of the present from the mysteries,
> the wraiths and shifts of time sense Wanstead Park held
> suspended,
> without remembering your eyes. Even when we were estranged
> And my own eyes smarted with pain and anger at the thought of
> you.
> And by other streams in other countries, anywhere where the
> light
> reaches down through shallows to gold gravel. Olga's
> brown eyes. . . .

Here is no argument, but by the subtlest associations past and present, change and permanence, the specific and the universal come to-

gether—freighted with the most personal meaning and made available to us by that loving recollection, "Olga's brown eyes." In a fashion which recalls but does not imitate the "turn" of traditional elegy, the announcement that the loved one lives in a new form, Denise Levertov brings together those "other streams in other countries," the light reaching down to gold gravel, to create a mood of unity with the world and with her sister. In this context she can speak of their estrangement and face frankly the most terrible facts about her sister's life, not because they are now explained but because the mystery of this other life has been taken into her own, to enlarge and nourish it.

> . . .Through the years of humiliation,
> of paranoia and blackmail and near starvation, losing
> the love of those you loved, one after another,
> parents, lovers, children, idolized friends, what kept
> compassion's candle alight in you, that lit you
> clear into another chapter (but the same book) 'a clearing
> in the selva oscura,
> a house whose door
> swings open, a hand beckons
> in welcome'?
>   I cross
> so many brooks in the world, there is so much light
> dancing on so many stones, so many questions my eyes
> smart to ask of your eyes, gold brown eyes,
> the lashes short but the lids
> arched as if carved out of olivewood, eyes with some vision
> of festive goodness in back of their hard, or veiled, or shining,
> unknowable gaze. . .

The final poem of "The Sorrow Dance" section, "To Speak," moves from lamentation to speech, from darkness to light, from the closed world to a new opening, from underground to the surface. Gathering up the themes and key words of the whole section, it confirms passage through a time of testing to a new endurance.

The disjunction of inner and outer life of which she speaks here she shows us, with authority, in these poems. She does not repudiate one of those worlds to live without tension in the other; she acknowledges the anguish of knowing both of them out of synchronization.

>   I have seen
> not behind but within, within the
> dull grief, blown grit, hideous

concrete façades, another grief, a gleam
as of dew, an abode of mercy,
have heard not behind but within noise
a humming that drifted into a quiet smile.

("City Psalm")

The insight stands by itself, not to be doubted, not expected to transform the horror and grief of life. Everything becomes transparent, revealing "an otherness that was blessed, that was bliss./*I saw Paradise in the dust of the street.*" The valuing of holiness and the capacity to abide with a mystery, qualities which marked Denise Levertov's earliest poetry, run much deeper as influences in the poetry of *The Sorrow Dance.* Emotions and words are tough and knotty; the poetry shows a distrust of aestheticizing raw emotions.

The images for the inner world in "Life at War" reveal some of the changes which the poet is undergoing in understanding the holy. One inner world is that of the "Didactic Poem," a world of dark, vampire-like spirits. Another represented by body fluids, "the mucous membrane of our dreams," "husky phlegm," struggles to throw off the corruption of the first. The war is the outward sign of this inner depravity, it is "the knowledge that jostles for space/in our bodies. . . ."

> We have breathed the grits of it in, all our lives,
> our lungs are pocked with it,
> the mucous membrane of our dreams
> coated with it, the imagination
> filmed over with the grey filth of it: . . .

"Life at War" refers not only to what it feels like to be alive when a war is going on, in Denise Levertov's hands that experience broadens out to describe what it means when the self is at war *with* itself. The Closed World becomes an encysted world. She emphasizes the point in "Second Didactic Poem" by describing our task as making "the honey of the human." Again biological action symbolizes the activity of a healthy inner life. The honey of man is being " 'more ourselves'/in the making," a process of "selving," in Hopkins's fine word. Corruption, dirt, virulence, the extraneous can all be turned to "Nectar,/the makings of the incorruptible," if the creature itself is healthy.

> enclosed and capped
> with wax, the excretion
> of bees' abdominal glands.
> Beespittle, droppings, hairs

of beefur: all become honey.
Virulent micro-organisms cannot
survive in honey.
          The taste,
the odor of honey:
each has no analogue but itself.

Our gathering, containing, working, "active in ourselves," creates that honey which has no analogues. In this extended metaphor, Denise Levertov has given us an image of individuation—the more powerful because it plays off against so many other images of life at war.

The decay of language and vision which operates as a major thematic thread in *The Sorrow Dance* finds expression both explicitly and in the montagelike, deliberately unfinished forms she employs in *Relearning the Alphabet.* Particularly in "An Interim" and "From a Notebook: October '68—May '69," two long poems which, with "Relearning the Alphabet," dominate the book, she borrows heavily from newspaper stories, letters, journal entries to give a documentary—and fragmentary—quality.

The titles tell a story: "Despair," "Tenebrae," "Wanting the Moon," "Not to Have," "A Defeat," "Craving," "Mad Song," "A Hunger." So do fragments and clipped sentences which make up stanzas and whole poems. "If I should find my poem is deathsongs./If I should find it has ended, when I looked for the next step."

The vision of unity rests on a kind of innocence, but in these poems both innocence and knowledge are a kind of damnation. She pictures a Black boy grabbing armfuls of gladioli in the Detroit Riots of 1967, but her imagination can do nothing with the picture, so the boy stands there, like a daydream whose action we cannot control, "useless knowledge in my mind's eye." She repeats "Biafra, Biafra, Biafra," to enlarge the "small stock of compassion/grown in us by the imagination," "trying to make room for more knowledge in my bonemarrow," but again the imagination fails, for she can find nothing to do.

In place of the easy inspiration of her earlier poems, that assurance of the connectedness of things, the unity between life and poems, there is now hunger, "a longing silent at song's core." Useless knowledge is guilty knowledge, what the traditional phrase means by "knowledge of sin." It presents itself as burden, loss of motive, existential distrust, "useless longing." The organic relationship between language and reality—so important to Denise Levertov—can no longer be assumed.

THE INNER WAR

O language, mother of thought,
are you rejecting us as we reject you?

Language, coral island
accrued from human comprehensions,
human dreams,

you are eroded as war erodes us.

In place of the old singleness of vision—which allowed "nakedness"
of language and innocent inspiration—the poet sees with fractured
vision, "multiple vision." "Advent 1966" speaks out of that multiple
vision, contrasting Southwell's vision of the Burning Babe, "prefigur-
ing/the Passion upon the Eve of Christmas," with our vision of the
burned children of Vietnam, "as off a beltline, more, more senseless
figures aflame." Christ's suffering redeems—"furnace in which souls are
wrought into new life"—but the multiple, repeated suffering of the
children damns.

Because in Vietnam the vision of a Burning Babe
is multiplied, multiplied,
                    the flesh on fire
not Christ's, as Southwell saw it, prefiguring
the passion upon the Eve of Christmas,

but wholly human and repeated, repeated,
infant after infant, their names forgotten,
their sex unknown in the ashes,
set alight, flaming but not vanishing,
not vanishing as his vision but lingering,

cinders upon the earth or living on
moaning and stinking in hospitals three abed;

because of this my strong sight,
my clear caressive sight, my poet's sight I was given
that it might stir me to song,
is blurred.

The suspended phrases, lingering over the gift of sight, fall to the
harshness of "blurred." Nightmare images follow: a cataract filming
over the inner eyes, a monstrous insect possessing one and looking out
through the eye-sockets "with multiple vision." Sight remains strong
and clear—"the insect/is not there, what I see is there"—but there is
nothing for the sight to caress.

Her vision is still single, then, in that it perceives an inherent order in things, but it has enlarged to include a profound awareness of evil. In the seven-part poem, "An Interim," she contrasts the harmony of the natural world with the disorder of America and the tensions surrounding her husband's acts of resistance to the Vietnam War. "An Interim" is one exercise of several in the book probing the deepest psychological and moral problem of the radical dissenter—how to translate resistance to what he perceives as all-pervasive evil into a positive peace. Many things may support the dissenter—adherence to a clear moral code, companionship with like-minded people, outrage, but also paranoia and hatred. The poem evolves around two definitions of peace, peace represented by nature—"Peace as grandeur. Energy/serene and noble."—and peace defined by the spiritual effect of its opposite—"The soul dwindles sometimes to an ant/rapid upon a cracked surface."

Inner peace cannot come to the resister unless he has first experienced that soul-dwindling. Like the poet, his work is to repossess the soul, but that can only be done by larger acts of restoration, including restoring virtue to language by making words accord with deeds. So the poet tests her way from one to another model of resistance, counterpointing passages praising the grandeur of ocean and sun with news accounts of a noncooperator's prison fast, reflections on the self-immolation of "the great savage saints of outrage" who burned themselves, diary entries and excerpts from the poet's letters concerning her husband's impending trial. She rejects none of the models, but affirms as her own, working "to make from outrage/islands of compassion others could build on." Of such resisters she says, "Their word if good,/ language draws breath again in their *yes* and *no*,/true testimony of love and resistance."

The poem represents an attempt to regain organic form—in life more than in literary creation—not a successful discovery of form. Overcoming her "cramp of fury" leads her into diffuse and flat writing. Yet we feel behind what is more a sketch for a poem than a finished work the regaining of perspective, a renewed trust in the virtue of language and the virtue of men.

"From a Notebook: October '68—May '69" pursues the same impressionistic method, gathering up phrases of poetry, fragments from reading, distant and recent memories, intense experiences into a notebook-poem which explores the choice, "Revolution or death." This exploration proceeds on several levels—the political and social are the most obvious, but the deepest and most influential is the personal, signaled by the weaving of nineteenth century poems about death into the fabric of her reflections. Moving into middle age has been an important theme in both *The Sorrow Dance* and *Relearning the Alphabet*; in "From a Notebook" the question of the old labor song, *"Which side are you on?"* refers not only to the choice indicated by "Revolution or death" but also by the contrast between the world of the young and that of the aging. At stake is learning how to live the second half of a life, how to grow as a poet.

The poem circles its subjects, exemplifying in its method what it "discovers" as its conclusion: that revolution must not be merely circular and life not merely linear, but that both must radiate from a center.

The rhythm of the opening section is set by the repeated phrase "Revolution or death," which acts on us as though the throb of train wheels repeated it. Working into that rhythm are those suggested by *"Which side are you on?"* and the biblical question "What makes this night different from all other nights?" Everything speaks of choice: choosing a side, being of the chosen people, choosing life with the young, because "Death is Mayor Daley." Death is also *"Unlived life/of which one can die."* Revolution is identified with "prismatic radiance pulsing from live tissue," and with resisters "blowing angel horns at the imagined corners," pronouncing a benediction over the world in an image borrowed from John Donne.

A counterstatement follows in the second section. Death is not only "the obscene sellout," it is also lovely and soothing. Over against this, the image of the pulsing brain:

> The will to live
> pulses.   Radiant emanations
> of living tissue, visible only
> to some photo-eye we know
> sees true because mind's dream-eye,
> inward gage, confirms it.
> Confirmation,
> a sacrament.

"How to live and the will to live," "revolution or death," objects, events, memories cluster around an unknown, shifting center which gives them "a character that throughout all transformations/reveals them connatural." Her life, seen as the tension of opposites, is also centered around something to which the opposites relate.

Enantiodromia, the being torn apart by opposites, which Jung speaks of as the problem of the mature person, aptly describes both the polarization one sees in American society and the conflicts within the self that Denise Levertov has explored since *The Sorrow Dance.* "Revolution or death" speaks simultaneously of the political and the psychic life.

Language again serves as a symbol for what is happening to the poet. Her roots are in the nineteenth century, so she is out of touch with those she most wants to know. Though she chooses revolution her words do not reach forward into it. "Language itself is my one home, my Jerusalem," but in this age of refugees she too has been uprooted.

> My diction marks me
> untrue to my time;
> change it, I'd be
> untrue to myself.

Part II is not "a going beyond" but a return and reexamination of themes. It is a meditation on revolution itself, which she describes as a new life, as like the secret uprising of the moon, as pervasive as "odor of snow,/freshwater,/stink of dank/vegetation recomposing."

Her husband, an intransigent pacifist friend, A. J. Muste become human symbols of resistance, revolution, and peace-making, both because of their own individual integrity and because the fullest human life is only a beginning.

What people can do together, as in the making of the People's Park in Berkeley, also symbolizes the revolution. "The War/comes home to us . . ." she says, when the People's Park is seized by the police. In the action of clearing the land, however, she has seen "poets and dreamers studying/joy together," finding in the cleared land a New World,

> each leaf of
> the new grass near us
> a new testament . . . .

The revolution she finally affirms is like a force of nature: a tree rising out of a flood, a sea full of swimmers, islands—like the islands of compassion in "In the Interim"—"which step out of the waves on rock feet."

"Relearning the Alphabet" recapitulates the book, gathering up its dominant themes, words, and images and making them the milestones of a journey from anguish back to "the ah! of praise." The device which shapes the poem, patterning it on the ABC books of childhood, allows many rich influences to operate. The organization is, on the surface, simple and arbitrary, since the sequence in which we learn the letters of the alphabet has no significance in itself, yet it is as absolute as numeral order. This is a quest-poem, however, and quests also move from point to point in what first appears to be an arbitrary sequence but eventually stands out as a necessary order where each test prepares us for the next. To relearn the alphabet requires going back to first things, to childhood.

"Relearning the Alphabet" is a poem of exploration, retracing an inner landscape which corresponds to the outward landscape—Vietnam, Biafra, Boston, Milwaukee, Berkeley, Maine—over which the other poems have ranged. What has been sought, or mourned, in those poems—joy, the moon, inspiration—is sought here.

It is also a recapitulation of her poetic life, gathering phrases and references from several of her own poems and from other poets, Hasidic tales, and fairy tales. In form the poem is also a recapitulation; she has relearned the alphabet by trying its sounds.

The poem begins in broken phrases, words displayed together kaleidescopically, but they touch on the stages of the quest: joy to be found in the extremes of anguish and ardor; to be relearned as unthinking knowledge; to be protected and fed with anguish and ashes.

> Joy—a beginning. Anguish, ardor.
> To relearn the ah! of knowing in unthinking
> joy: the beloved stranger lives.
> Sweep up anguish as with a wing-tip,
> brushing the ashes back to the fire's core.

"The fire's core" runs through the poem as a signature for the contrarieties of joy, changing and enlarging in meaning as the poet appropriates more of her experiences and insights into the framework offered by alphabetical order.

Hoping and wanting are important, but they make nothing happen. Being open, following the leading, are all the quester has. She has guides on her quest, but they lead by misdirection and by making her stumble. When she is "called forth" by a question, she only knows what she was unable to find:

A POETRY OF EXPLORATION

> Lost in the alphabet
> I was looking for
> the word I can't now say

(love)

But the calling forth occurred through the love in a question, and suddenly she finds herself home again, back from the false quests.

> I am trusted, I trust
> the real that transforms me.
> And relinquish
> in grief
> *the seeing that burns through, comes through*
> *to fire's core:* transformation, continuance,
> as acts of magic I would perform, are no longer
> articles of faith.

False quests are those we will ourselves to make—wanting the moon. Being "called forth" depends on letting go, relinquishing what is most precious to the will. The whole book has been concerned with holding onto or recapturing vision and joy, or satisfying hunger and longing. It has been marked by distrust of former innocence, near-repudiation of former simplicity and easy inspiration. But always she has wanted confirmation of her past, "transformation, continuance," and many of the poems have fought through to magnificently enlarged vision, still rooted in "imagination's holy forest" as she had known it. In "Relearning the Alphabet" the final relinquishment occurs, the recognition that "acts of magic" and "articles of faith" are "rules of the will—graceless/faithless," and that she must yield all desire, all yearning for vision or wisdom, before the treasure will disclose itself. And the treasure is a new trust, a recognition that holiness *is*, both in the world and in the self.

> Relearn the alphabet,
> relearn the world, the world
> understood anew only in doing, under-
> stood only as
> looked-up-into out of earth,
> the heart an eye looking,
> the heart a root
> planted in earth.
> Transmutation is not
> under the will's rule.

Everything the poet wanted has been given, but neither in the form nor with the meaning she had willed. Confirmation, joy, the fire's core—she has gained each through the making of poetry. *Relearning the Alphabet* represents a completion and a new beginning. In her "Statement on Poetics" in 1959, Denise Levertov had said, "Insofar as poetry has a social function it is to awaken sleepers by other means than shock." In her last two books we are aware of the terrible shocks she has sustained and the struggle she has passed through to regain or earn her eloquence. "All utterance/takes me step by hesitant step towards/ —yes, to continuance: into/that life beyond the dead-end where/. . .I was lost."

We find a new sophistication in her understanding of what it means to be "members one of another." It has consequences for political action, from making a people's park to conspiring against "illegitimate authority." That enlarged understanding has brought new subjects to her poetry and an enlarged practice in writing "organic" poetry. The inherent form behind things, the truth, has been sought through montage and documentary. The poetry which results sometimes seems extravagant, rough, or unfinished. But we trust it because we trust the life it comes out of and the sense of holiness which inspires Denise Levertov to write.